Musical Instruments of the West

A.M.D.G.

To
MY MOTHER
and to the memory of
MY FATHER

Musical Instruments of the West

MARY REMNANT

B.T. Batsford Limited
London

First published 1978

Copyright Mary Remnant 1978

Filmset in Monophoto Sabon by
Servis Filmsetting Ltd, Manchester
Printed in Great Britain by
The Anchor Press Ltd, Tiptree
for the publishers B.T. Batsford Ltd,
4 Fitzhardinge Street, London W1H 0AH

ISBN 0 7134 0569 4

Contents

Illustrations

The jacket illustration, from *Theatrum Sanitatis, MS.4182 f.200, Biblioteca Casanatense, Rome,* is by courtesy of *Scala, Florence.*

Acknowledgements for pictures are given in italics. The author is most grateful to the authorities concerned.

Preface

The purpose of this book is to provide a basic historical outline of the instruments used in western art music, illustrating it as fully as a reasonable price will allow, and, as far as possible, using pictures which have not hitherto appeared in similar works.

Due to its concise nature, it avoids much detail and has no footnotes. The Bibliography points to more specialized writings, and these in turn refer to works in languages other than English, besides numerous relevant articles in such periodicals as the *Galpin Society Journal*. Most of the quotations in the text, e.g. those from Tinctoris, Burney, etc., can be traced through the General section of the Bibliography. From the following less obvious sources are taken the quotations on the pages indicated:

Baines, Anthony: 'Two Cassel Inventories', *GSJ IV* (1951), pp. 30–37. Quotation on p. 131.

Gai, Vinicio: *Gli Strumenti Musicali della Corte Medicea e il Museo del Conservatorio 'Luigi Cherubini' di Firenze*, Florence, 1969, p. 11. Quotation (translated) on p. 87.

Galpin, Canon Francis W.: *Old English Instruments of Music*, 4th edn., rev. Thurston Dart, London, 1965. Appendix 4, 'The Musical Instruments of King Henry VIII'. Quotations on pp. 37, 58, 102, 117, 119, 179.

Ecorcheville, J.: 'Quelques Documents sur la Musique de la Grande Ecurie du Roi', *SIMG*, pp. 608ff. Quotation on p. 208.

Rickert, Edith: *Chaucer's World*: ed. Clair C. Olson, Martin M. Crow and Margaret Rickert, London, 1948, pp. 75, 342. Quotations on pp. 115, 170.

Kelly, Michael: *Solo Recital*, ed. Herbert van Thal, introd. by J.C. Trewin, London, 1972, p. 227. Quotation on p. 89.

Marcuse, Sibyl: 'The Instruments of the King's Library at Versailles', *GSJ* XIV (1961), 34–6. Quotation on p. 126.

Ord-Hume, Arthur W.J.G.: *Clockwork Music*, London, 1973, p. 298. Quotation on p. 184.

Perrot, Jean: *The Organ . . . to the end of the Thirteenth Century*, transl. Norma Deane, London, New York, Toronto, 1971, pp. 127, 129. Quotations on pp. 121, 135 (Dio Chrysostom), 192.

Russell, Raymond: *The Harpsichord and Clavichord*, 2nd edn. rev. Howard Schott, London, 1973, p. 25. Quotation on p. 78.

Many people have helped in one way or another towards the completion of this book, and my grateful thanks go to all of them. In particular there should be mentioned the following from the Royal College of Music: Sir Keith Falkner, the former Director; Sir David Willcocks, the present Director; Mrs Elizabeth Wells, the Curator of the Museum of Instruments; the Librarians; Mrs Sylvia Latham, Miss Joan Littlejohn, and other members of the present staff, besides my pupils there during the last 7 years, who have given me much food for thought.

Others include Miss Elizabeth Agate, Mr Anthony Baines, Mr James Blades, Professor Giles Brindley, Mr Ralph Downes, Mr Michael Graham-Dixon, Frau Uta Henning, Mrs Annetta Hoffnung, M. Hohner Ltd., Mrs Carleen Hutchins, Dr Robert Sherlaw Johnson, Miss Sheila Lawrence, Mr John Leach, Mr Frank Merrick, Mr John Morton, Mr Leslie Orrey, Percussion Services Ltd., Professor Gilbert Reaney, Mr E.A.K. Ridley, The Royal Military School of Music, Dr Stanley Sadie, Dr Silio Italico Sarpi, Dr Howard Schott, Dr Frederick Sternfeld, and Signora Livia Zanini Barilli. Their contributions to the book have been invaluable, and all its deficiencies are my own.

The book as it is could not have come about without the help of Mr Samuel Carr and Mrs Celia Hollis of B.T. Batsford Ltd., together with that of Mr David Higham. To them, to the Royal Musical Association which has contributed towards the photographic expenses, and to the Winston Churchill Memorial Trust which in 1967 gave me a Travelling Fellowship to study instruments abroad, I owe a special debt of gratitude.

Finally there is my mother, who has been a constant source of help and encouragement during the years involved in this book. Those who know her will realize how fortunate I am.

MARY REMNANT
London, August 1977

ABBREVIATIONS USED IN THE TEXT

GSJ   Galpin Society Journal
SIMG Sammelbände der Internationalen Musikgesellschaft

Introduction

It is easy to become absorbed by the subject of musical instruments, whether we are performers, teachers, students, or those most important people, the members of the audience. Some are interested in old instruments, some in new, others in folk instruments, and many, the author included, have an obsession for finding instruments in the visual arts, as well as for playing them. The result of all this is that today more instruments are being made, more knowledge is coming to light about their past, and more useful pictures are being discovered than at any previous period in history.

The subject, however, is so vast, that only a small part of it can be written in any one book. It has been decided, therefore, to restrict this short account mainly to those instruments which were, and are, involved in the art music of the West. Certain folk instruments of today are referred to in passing, but however important they may be, they are not normally treated as separate items. Classification has been kept to a minimum, each chapter being built round instruments with similar methods of playing or construction, and where possible following the families of the orchestra. It has not been possible to include the numerous hybrids, particularly if no repertoire exists for them. Nor has it been possible to describe or to illustrate the limitless varieties and different tunings among instruments which were never standardized, particularly those from before 1500.

From this early period very few actual instruments survive, so for evidence we have to rely on the visual arts, on various forms of literature, and on expense accounts. The matter of artistic licence or error is of great concern, the final test being whether or not the instrument portrayed could work. If it could not, the reason is either that the artist did not know enough, or that he never intended to be scrupulously accurate, as is indicated clearly by the more fanciful designs. Sometimes a correct instrument is held in an unplayable position for the sake of pictorial symmetry, or else purely for convenience. An angel in a church roof, for instance, may have to point his instrument downwards for it to be seen at all clearly from below, while a carved instrument close to the ground, as on a misericord, may be held in an adapted position to avoid being broken. If, however, artistic licence or error are plain in one or two details, this does not necessarily mean that the whole instrument is wrong. On a wider scale the same principle can be applied to instrumental *ensembles*. The pictorial grouping together of certain

15

instruments need not be dismissed as unlikely just because one of them has the wrong number of strings or fingerholes. Over all these problems we have to use our discretion, as also on the subject of musicians who are shown, not as human beings, but as angels, animals, devils or grotesques. In the Middle Ages particularly, minstrels often dressed up to perform, whether for religious drama, for a village fair, or for the jollifications of a noble court, and the visual artist often portrayed what he had seen in real life. Even when a picture of angel musicians represents nothing more than a picture of angel musicians, the playing together of their particular instruments may give valuable evidence of performance practice.

Terminology must also be treated with care. While one instrument can be known by several different names, the converse is also true, one word being applied to several instruments. Certain words, such as *lute, fiddle* and *horn*, are used generically to cover a whole class of instruments, but they can also mean one type in particular. As with artistic licence, so is poetic licence a hazard, a striking example being in the mediaeval word *rote* which seems to have been used by some poets with no particular image in mind except that it rhymed with *note*. On the whole, mediaeval authors referred to instruments of their own time when writing about a past age. Robert Manning of Brunne, for instance, in *The Story of England*, described the celebrations at the court of King Arthur as being enlivened by the fourteenth-century instruments which he himself knew. More recently, writers of historical novels have tended to refer to mediaeval instruments by Renaissance names, while the ways in which Biblical instruments have been translated through the ages is the subject for a book in itself. Suffice it to say that only recently have real attempts been made to use words really representative of the instruments played by the Hebrews.

Surviving instruments themselves can be misleading, as over the years many have been altered. Lutes have been made into hurdy-gurdies, harpsichords have been enlarged and had their original pitch changed by as much as a fourth, and the celebrated gittern now in the British Museum was several hundred years ago turned into a 'violin', and given a false back inside. Already in the Baroque era certain instruments were faked to look older, and given the name of an already famous maker together with a fictitious date – only foreshadowing the numerous school violins which today bear the inscription *Antonio Stradivari*.

Related to this is the 'restoration' of art works, a notable example being the thirteenth-century painted roof of Peterborough Cathedral, where nineteenth-century activities blatantly turned a mediaeval fiddle into a violin, complete with a Tourte-style bow. Repainted carvings fare better if they retain their original shape, and the making of plaster casts, such as was done many years ago for the roof bosses in Tewkesbury Abbey, can add considerably to the knowledge of musicians and art historians alike. Fortunately there are now a good many restorers of art works and instruments who go to great trouble to return an object to its original appearance, while placing on record just what their work has involved.

Finally, a word about performance, without which no instruments would have been made. The great interest today in history of all kinds has brought about a desire to hear music played as nearly as possible to its original sounds. Surviving instruments which are still in good playing condition can give us these at once, while others can provide the basis for reconstructions. When there are few or no instruments available, as from the mediaeval period, we must rely more than ever on the visual arts and on literature, which tell us, not only about the instruments themselves, but also about their groupings and the social conditions in which they were played. The angels, devils, animals and grotesques must help us to re-create the music of their own time.

MATTERS OF PITCH

Throughout the text, specific notes will be written in italics, while keys in general, and notes at no specific octave, will be in plain capital letters.

FIG. 1 shows

a) the pitch name for each octave, written below the bass clef and above the treble clef;

b) the length in feet of an open diapason organ pipe at each C, written between the staves.

(When the C pipe is 8′ long, the keyboard produces the same pitch as that of the piano. When it is 4′ long the sound is an octave higher, and when 16′ long, an octave lower.)

FIG. 2. The *Harmonic Series*, showing the fundamental note (in the key of C) and its overtones.

*The 11th harmonic is slightly sharp, and the 13th slightly flat.

18

— CHAPTER I —
Stringed Instruments –
Plucked

1. Kithara, played in a song contest depicted on an Attic vase, *c.*500 BC. *Kassel, Staatliche Kunstsammlungen.*

Since the unknown time when Man discovered that strings of varying material, thickness and length could give forth different musical notes, he has experimented with ways of producing and increasing their sounds. The resulting instruments, described today as *chordophones*, can be classified generically as lyres, harps, zithers and lutes, and their different sounds can be obtained by plucking, striking, rubbing or bowing. Because of their great antiquity, the plucked instruments will be treated first.

The family of **lyres** is characterized by a yoke, which connects two arms rising from the soundbox below. The strings, which are more or less of equal length, are fixed to the lower part of the instrument, and continue up to the yoke, where they are adjusted. The earliest types were mainly of wood, and some, such as those excavated in the 'Royal Cemetery' at Ur (*c*.2500 BC), had inlaid patterns or were covered with silver. These 'box-lyres', which include the Hebrew **kinnor** of the Psalms and the **kithara** of classical Greece and Rome, were among the most important instruments of Antiquity. The early mediaeval **cruit, chrotta** or **rotta** which emerged from the Dark Ages was basically of this type, varying in shape as did its forbears, and in its simplest form being almost rectangular, as indicated by the remains of the seventh-century lyre discovered at Sutton Hoo in Suffolk. The Bible of Charles the Bald (Paris, Bibliothèque Nationale, MS Lat. I, f.215v.) shows a lyre with a central neck enabling the performer to obtain more sounds by stopping the strings against it with his fingers.

The **lyra** of the Greeks developed later than the kithara, with its origins steeped in legend. One story is that the infant god Hermes, on an expedition to steal 50 of

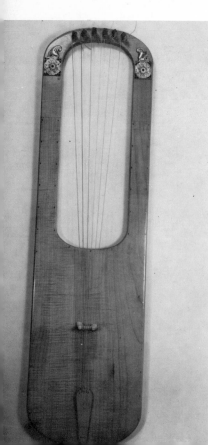

Apollo's heifers, picked up a tortoise shell, stretched ox hide over it, and attached to it seven gut strings. When the enraged Apollo traced the thief he was calmed by the sound of the new instrument, and after being presented with it by Hermes, became known as the god of music. Whatever the truth of the matter, this lyre often had a resonator of tortoise shell covered with a skin belly, and is described as a 'bowl-lyre'. Its arms and yoke were of wood, and, like the kithara, it was plucked by a plectrum, in contrast to the more ancient types and the mediaeval lyres, which were normally plucked by the fingers. After its long and distinguished history the lyre family passed out of the main stream of art music during the Middle Ages, due to the greater potentialities of the harp, but in folk music it can still be found today, notably in Scandinavia among European countries.

Among the earliest sources of the **harp** (in which the plane of the strings is perpendicular to the soundboard) are carvings from the Aegean Islands dating from the third millennium BC. While the later pre-Christian Greeks certainly knew the harp, they and the Romans preferred the lyre types, as did the minstrels of the early Middle Ages. It was only from the Romanesque period onwards that the harp permanently gained precedence in Europe. This was the type known as the 'frame harp', in which the string arm and soundchest, holding respectively the upper and lower ends of the strings, are joined by a front pillar (which was, and still is, often absent from non-European harps). The mediaeval frame was frequently made of willow, and occasionally of ivory, and its strings could be of gut, metal or twisted hair. The Norman Welsh chronicler Giraldus Cambrensis (Gerald de Barri, *c.*1146–*c.*1220) tells us in his *Topographia Hibernica* that the

2. (Far Left) Reconstruction of an early mediaeval lyre (chrotta) based on the 7th-century fragments excavated at Sutton Hoo. *London, British Museum.*

3. (Left) Lyra, played by Nike. Detail from a red-figured oil-flask by the Pan painter, *c.*490 BC. *Oxford, Ashmolean Museum.*

4. (Right) Harp-player, sculpted in the Aegean Islands in the 3rd millennium BC. *New York, Metropolitan Museum, Rogers Fund.*

5. Harp, played by David to Saul. Detail from an English Psalter, *c.*1225. *New York, Pierpont Morgan Library, MS. G.25, f.3v.*

Irish used 'strings made of brass instead of skin' ('Aeneis quoque utuntur chordis, non de corio factis'), while the thirteenth-century Franciscan Bartholomaeus Anglicus, in his *De Proprietatibus Rerum* (*c.*1230), says that strings of sheep and wolf gut should not be mixed:

> strengis made of guttes of wolves destroyeþ and fretiþ and corrumpiþ strengis made of guttis of schiepe ȝif hit so be þat þey beþ so sette among them as in fethele or in harpe . . .

(Translation by John of Trevisa, 1398/9. British Library MS Add. 27944, f.142v.) The thirteenth-century romance *King Horn* describes a harp being played with 'nayles scharpe', a method which survived for several hundred years in Ireland, where harpers continued to grow long fingernails.

By the end of the Middle Ages the harp varied to different degrees between two main types. The Irish harp was massively built, having a wide soundchest of willow, a distinctive front pillar, and metal strings. Similar instruments were used in other parts of the British Isles, and several have survived. In contrast, the 'Gothic' harp of the Continent, such as would have been played by the Dukes of Burgundy Philip the Good and his son Charles the Bold, had a narrower frame and soundchest, and normally gut strings. (Many harps at this time had 'brays'; these were L-shaped metal pins which held the strings to the soundchest, strengthened the sound, and produced a somewhat buzzing effect.) Then came a crisis. Because the harp was tuned in advance to suit the key of each piece of music, it could not cope with the increasing chromaticism of the late fifteenth century, and gave way in importance to the fretted lute, on which all the semitones could be played. While diatonic harps were still made, they became restricted to simple and traditional music in which the instrument did not need to modulate during performance.

To retain its place in the history of art music, the harp therefore had to become chromatic, and the sixteenth century produced a solution. This was the **double harp** or **arpa doppia**, which had a row of chromatic strings alongside the diatonic ones, as can be seen in a beautiful Italian example of the period, now kept at the Galleria Estense, Modena. (Plate 6, however, shows that some form of double harp was already known in Spain before 1400, but nothing is known of its tuning.) The **triple harp**, which, according to Marin Mersenne's *Harmonie Universelle* (1636) was invented *c.*1600 by the Neapolitan 'Sieur Luc Anthoine Eustache', had three rows of strings, the outer ones being diatonic and played by one hand to each, while the inner one was chromatic and played by either hand. Having survived longest in Wales, it is now called the 'Welsh harp'.

Meanwhile, seventeenth-century experiments in Bavaria and the Tyrol resulted in a single-strung harp in which certain strings were equipped with a hook at the top end. Each hook when twisted would tighten a string to raise it by a semitone, but as this could only be done by a hand which was not playing, chromatic changes were impossible during fast passages involving both hands. This problem was resolved in the **pedal harp**, attributed to one Hochbrucker of Donauwörth in Bavaria, *c.*1720. By means of wires or rods inside the front pillar, the hooks were connected to pedals at the bottom of the soundchest. By pressing one pedal down to a notch, all the Cs were raised, by pressing the next pedal all the Ds, etc., although at first this applied only to certain notes. After a time seven pedals were used, so that all the notes could be changed, and to accommodate the connecting links inside, the front pillar was now regularly straightened. Parisian makers then tried new types of hook, known as *crochets, béquilles* and *fourchettes* (describing their respective shapes of hooks, crutches and forks), to ease the manner of tightening the strings. Sébastien Erard, who invented the *fourchettes*, later devised a second row of them, together with an extra notch for each pedal, thus raising the pitch of a string by another semitone and enabling the performer to play in every key. (All the flats, naturals and sharps were now available, the natural position of each pedal being in the upper notch.) Having left France during the

6. Double harp and psaltery. Detail of a Spanish reliquary (*c.*1390) from the monastery of Piedra. *Madrid, Academia de la Historia.*

7. Welsh triple harp of the 19th century, played by Nansi Richards Jones. *Cardiff, Welsh Folk Museum, St Fagan's Castle.*

8. Single action harp with *crochets*, by H. Nadermann, Paris, after 1785. By means of an extra pedal, soundholes in its back could be covered or uncovered, thus producing a swell effect. *London, Victoria and Albert Museum.*

Revolution, Erard patented this 'double action' in London in 1810. He also made the strings tighter and thicker, strengthened the soundchest, and decorated the head and base of the pillar with Greek maidens and lyre-players, causing the instrument to be called the 'Grecian harp'. In 1836 his nephew Pierre Erard produced his own 'Gothic harp', identified by its angels and Gothic arches. Here the strings were further apart than before, and there were three extra ones, one in the treble and two in the bass. These, however, did not have pedals, which were finally added by Wilfrid Smith of London in 1958. The range of the concert harp is now from Cb' to gb''''.

The improvements made by Sébastien Erard greatly changed the position of the harp in society. The single action instruments of the Parisian families of Nadermann and Cousineau had been played, not only by professionals, but also by numerous amateurs including Queen Marie Antoinette of France, and many harps from this period remain to decorate the stately homes of Europe. The new instrument, being larger, heavier and more complicated to play, was too difficult for many harpists, who, recognizing its superior qualities, gave up the harp altogether for the piano. Such a musician was Dorette, wife of the violinist and composer Louis Spohr, who wrote many compositions for harp and violin. Berlioz, who made much use of the improved instrument in his compositions, was often frustrated by the lack of performers, but he was nevertheless able to muster 25 harpists to play together at a festival connected to the Paris Industrial Exhibition of 1844. Since 1889 the American firm of Lyon and Healy, and since 1909 that

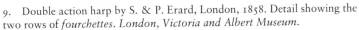

9.   Double action harp by S. & P. Erard, London, 1858. Detail showing the two rows of *fourchettes*. *London, Victoria and Albert Museum.*

10.   Monochord played by Boethius, in a 12th-century English MS. of his
De Musica. Cambridge University Library, MS. Ii.3.12, f.61v.

11.   (Right) Psaltery and gittern, from a margin of an English 14th-century
psalter. *London, British Library, MS. Ar.83, f.63v.*

of Wurlitzer, have further strengthened the instrument and made the mechanism smoother. Meanwhile there have been various attempts to produce a cross-strung chromatic harp without pedals, notably that by Pleyel, Wolff & Co. (1894), for which Debussy wrote his *Danse Sacrée et Danse Profane* (1904). Such instruments, however, could not replace the Erard harp.

Irish harping continued in its traditional manner until about 1800, by which time the European pedal harp had reached Ireland. Amateurs wishing to play on a more simple instrument were rewarded by the small 'Portable Irish Harp' produced by John Egan of Dublin *c.*1819, in which the work of pedals was achieved by single action blades set into the front pillar.

In contrast to the harp, the zither family consists of instruments in which the strings run parallel to the soundboard. One of the earliest examples was the **monochord**, said to have been invented by Pythagoras in the sixth century BC, and much used by mediaeval mathematicians. Its single plucked string changed in pitch as a bridge was moved beneath it from one marked point to another on the long and narrow soundboard. Its part, if any, in art music must have been very limited.

A more musical form of zither is the **psaltery**, which is of obscure origin and cannot with any certainty be identified as the 'psalterium' of the Vulgate. Triangular and quadrangular instruments were thus described in a much-reproduced letter said to be from St Jerome to a certain Dardanus, but this is now believed to have been forged in the ninth century. From that time onwards, however, these shapes are increasingly seen in other contexts, the triangular ones sometimes described as 'rota' or 'rotta', as can be seen on an eleventh-century capital in the cloisters of the abbey of Moissac, where one of David's minstrels is accompanied by the inscription CVM ROTA [Eman]. Such instruments, when they were actually used, may have consisted simply of a soundboard with supports beneath its edges, as illustrations do not normally show them to have the sound-holes which suggest the presence of a hollow box. Such holes appear in psalteries with increasing frequency from the twelfth century onwards, perhaps due to the influence of the Arabic *qānūn* which was then already known in Spain. Trapezoidal in shape, and with strings tuned three or four to a note, its characteristics were soon to be seen in other European psalteries, particularly those of the South. (Its name was also adopted, becoming *canon* in French and *canone* in Italian, with *micanon* and *mezzo canone* being used for instruments of half the normal shape.) In the North, an instrument with incurved sides and only one or two

strings to a note was preferred, one of its earliest depictions being in the Bodleian Library's twelfth-century English Psalter, MS Auct.D.2.8, f.88. In eastern Europe wing-shaped psalteries were given the Latin name *ala*, leading to the modern description **Bohemian wing**; in the same part of the world an instrument flourished which combined the soundboxes of both harp and psaltery, and today goes by the name of **psaltery-harp**. Psaltery strings were best made of brass or silver, according to the *Ars Musica* of the Spanish monk Johannes Aegidius Zamorensis, who lived in the thirteenth century. They were plucked either by the fingers or by quill plectra, the two methods being suitable for music of different moods, and the latter showing the instrument's direct ancestry of the harpsichord. Among the numerous references to the playing of the psaltery on occasions of celebration, is that from the fifteenth-century English romance *The Squire of Low Degree*:

> Ye shall have harpe, sautry, and songe,
> And other mirthes you amonge;
> Ye shall have rumney and malmesine,
> Both ypocrasse and vernage wine . . .

Like the harp, the psaltery was adversely affected by Renaissance chromaticism, and it gradually went out of favour, continuing mainly as a domestic instrument in such varied forms as the Germanic **Spitzharfe** or **double psaltery**, and as the **Bell Harp** invented soon after 1700 by John Simcock of Bath. The dulcimer, an

12.   Psaltery-harp. Detail from *The Coronation of the Virgin* by an anonymous German painter, *c*.1350. *Cologne, Wallraf-Richartz-Museum*.

13.   Scheitholt, played by one of many musical angels in the 16th-century wall paintings at *Rynkeby Church, Fuen, Denmark.*

offshoot of the psaltery, is to this day sometimes plucked as an alternative to its normal striking action (see p. 176), and the bell harp was often struck.

The specific meaning of the word **zither** applies to an offshoot of the psaltery which is little used in art music, but it deserves mention. In its earliest known form, the **Scheitholt**, it was long and narrow like the monochord, but had frets for diatonic notes on its soundboard. According to Praetorius (1619), its three or four brass strings could be tuned to the unison, fifth or octave, although the exact arrangement was variable. To play a tune, the performer pressed the strings against the frets by means of a small stick in his left hand, while his right thumb strummed on them near the bridge. As the frets stretched across the whole soundboard, the effect would have been somewhat reminiscent of parallel organum. Later forms of the instrument, however, had extra strings which were not stopped by the fingers, and were used to give a droning chordal accompaniment to the melody. The Scheitholt led to many different types of zither, its approximate shape being retained in the Hungarian *cithera* and the French *épinette des Vosges*. In Germanic countries, however, the soundbox was gradually extended to allow for a greater number of strings, and during the nineteenth century the instrument acquired its present forms. It now has chromatic frets, and about five melody strings which are plucked by a metal plectrum attached to the performer's right thumb. The unstopped strings have increased in number to over thirty, and are tuned in such a way that, by plucking with separate fingers of his right hand, the player can obtain different chords as required. Throughout its history, the zither has been used mainly for domestic and folk music, but recently it has also found a prominent place in films.

14.   Zither by Franz Nowy, Vienna, *c*.1950. *London, Collection of John Leach.*

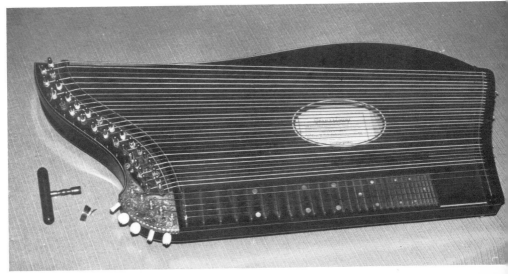

15. Lute (with four strings) and mandora. Detail from *The Coronation of the Virgin* by Agnolo Gaddi (*fl.* 1369–96). *Washington, National Gallery of Art, Samuel H. Kress Collection.*

The generic family of lutes consists of those instruments in which a neck proceeds from the body, and the performer presses the strings against it, or touches them above it with his fingers to obtain the notes required. Normally, those with vaulted backs are classified as 'lutes' and those with flat backs as 'guitars', but this is not an inflexible rule. While their history in Asia, northern Africa, Greece and Rome can be traced back to Antiquity, there is little evidence of these instruments in northern Europe before the early Middle Ages. Some of them, however, may have come north through the Byzantine influence, which was already strong before the Moors invaded Spain in 711, bringing their own instruments with them.

In its specific sense, the vaulted **lute** (the name comes from the Arabic *al-úd*, meaning 'the wood') was certainly established in Spain by the tenth century, but our knowledge of it in England only dates from *c.*1300. Its curved back may originally have been made from one piece of wood (particularly in the long-necked lutes played in southern Europe in the earlier part of the Middle Ages), but as the instrument grew larger this was replaced by ribs of hard wood such as maple or sycamore, and some late examples are of ivory and ebony. The soundboard or belly was of a softer wood, and contained open soundholes or, as in most cases, a carved rose. The gut strings passed from a frontal stringholder to a pegbox bent back at a right angle to the neck, which was short and, from the fourteenth century onwards, normally fitted with gut frets. (Before this time, frets seem to have been less frequent.) Early European lutes often had four single strings, apparently tuned to pitches relative to *c f a d'*, which were plucked with a plectrum. Then

16. Six-course Renaissance lute. Detail from wall-paintings by Garofalo, 1505–08. *Ferrara, Palazzo di Ludovico il Moro, Sala del Tesoro.*

17.   Theorbo by Michael Rauche, London, 1762. *London, Victoria and Albert Museum.*

18.   (Right) Chitarrone by Magnus Tieffenbrucker, Venice, 1608. *London, Royal College of Music.*

they became double (with the exception of the top string which remained single) and the pitch was extended, first upwards to *g'*, and then downwards to *G*, resulting in the fifteenth-century six-course lute attributed to the Germans by the Flemish writer Johannes Tinctoris in his *De inventione et usu musicae* (*c.*1487). He added that they sometimes reinforced the sound by making one string of each pair in brass, tuned an octave below the other. Also during this period there evolved the technique of plucking with the fingers, giving greater musical scope to the performer, and leading to an idiomatic lute style. According to Tinctoris

> . . . some teams will take the treble part of any piece you care to give them and improvize marvellously upon it with such taste that the performance cannot be rivalled. Among such, Pietro Bono (Avogari), lutenist to Ercole, Duke of Ferrara, is in my opinion pre-eminent.
>
> Furthermore, others will do what is much more difficult; namely to play a composition alone, and most skilfully, in not only two parts, but even in three or four. For example, Orbus the German, or Henri who was recently in the service of Charles, Duke of Burgundy: the German was super-eminent in playing in this way.

Soon afterwards there was established in Bologna a celebrated school of German lute-makers. Laux (Luca) Maler, who was living there from 1518, was the son of Conrad (Corrado) Maler, a lute-maker of 'Alemania alta'. When Laux died in 1552 he owned three shops, left 998 new lutes besides 127 incomplete ones, and his will referred to over 1000 soundboards. The Bologna school eventually passed to native Italian makers such as Girolamo Brensi, and was followed by similar centres at Padua, Venice and Rome.

19.   Theorbo-lute, held by *A Man with an Arch-lute*, attributed to I. Luttichuijs (1616–73). *Glasgow Art Gallery.*

As the pitch of individual instruments varied, lutenists played not from normal notation but from tablature, in which the stave represented the strings, and letters or numbers (according to the type of tablature in use) indicated the required frets. The appearance of lute tablature coincided approximately with the invention of printing, and the earliest lute music to appear in print was a collection of *ricercari* and song arrangements by Francesco Spinaccino, published by Ottaviano dei Petrucci at Venice in 1507.

With the increasing need for lower notes during the Renaissance period, there evolved the theorbo and chitarrone, both covered by the term 'archlute'. The **theorbo** had, not only six or more stopped strings (in early examples these were single – Samuel Pepys was one of many musicians who had his instrument adapted for double courses, in 1661), but also a set of longer and deeper strings attached to a second pegbox extending beyond the regular one in the same plane. These strings were not stopped by the fingers, and were tuned to the current needs of the performer. The **chitarrone** had a similar arrangement of strings, except that the stopped ones were almost always in double courses, each of the pair being tuned an octave apart, and they were often of brass. It had a longer neck than the theorbo, resulting in certain cases in a total length of seven feet. Both these instruments appeared in the sixteenth century, to be joined in the mid seventeenth by the **angelica** or **angel lute**, an archlute with about 16 strings which were tuned diatonically and therefore did not need to be stopped by the fingers. Because they were somewhat unwieldy, archlutes were used mainly for accompaniment, whether for a solo singer or instrumentalist, or in a group, and in orchestras they played continuo parts. During the seventeenth century there appeared also the **theorbo-lute**, which was double strung like the Renaissance lute, and had its right-angled pegbox, but had extra bass strings like the larger theorbo. Its tunings varied, to suit the demands of such composers as Denis and Ennemond Gaultier in France, and Esaias Reusner and Silvius Weiss in Germany. Although the lute was on the wane in the eighteenth century, it was called for in suites by J.S. Bach, concertos by Vivaldi, and chamber music by Haydn, while Dr Charles Burney, visiting Paris in 1770, heard 'M. Kohaut, who played very well, on the Arch Lute'. Meanwhile a long-necked lute of Asiatic style had appeared in Italy under the name **colascione**, but its use was restricted mainly to amateur music-making.

One of the smallest and narrowest forms of lute was known in Antiquity as the **pandora**. Occasional variants of it are seen in early mediaeval art, but not until the *Ars Nova* period was it frequently portrayed throughout Europe. By that time called **mandora** or **mandore**, it had a sickle-shaped pegbox often ending in a carved head, and its gut strings were plucked with a plectrum (see plate 15). Frets were normal by the late Middle Ages. Many mandoras have survived from the Renaissance and Baroque periods, when they were tuned in fifths and fourths, e.g. *c g c′ g′ c″*. Since then the chief developments have been in Italy, where the instrument varied according to district under the name **mandolino**. The Milanese type (which was not restricted to Italy) represented the culmination of the mandora, keeping its pairs of gut strings and frontal stringholder, while the Neapolitans preferred metal strings tuned to *g d′ a′ e″* as on the violin, with the

20. Pandora, in a statuette from Tanagra, 3rd century BC. *Paris, Musée du Louvre.*

21. Mandoras by (top) Joseph Molinari, Venice, 1757, and (bottom) Jean Nicolas Lambert, Paris, 1752 (?). *London, Victoria and Albert Museum.*

strings passing over a low bridge to be attached to pins on the back. The bass mandolin was often known as **mandola** or **mandolone**. While it did not become a regular member of the orchestra, the mandolin has from time to time appeared with it for special effects. Vivaldi wrote concertos for it, Mozart used it for a serenade in *Don Giovanni,* and Beethoven wrote pieces for it with pianoforte. Burney, in an eye-witness account of the welcome given in Brescia to the native singer Luini Bonetto, on his return in 1770 from Russia, wrote

> He was welcomed home by a band of music . . . consisting of two violins, a mandoline, french horn, trumpet, and violon-cello; and, though in the dark, they played long concertos, with solo parts for the mandoline.

Instruments of the guitar family, with parallel or incurved sides and generally with a flat back, are often seen in European art from the thirteenth century onwards. Before that time they are less frequent, passing back through Romanesque examples of Spain and Italy (e.g. at the Palace of Archbishop Gelmirez at Santiago de Compostela, and in the Baptistery at Parma) to the Stuttgart Psalter of *c.*830 (Plate 76), and clearly foreshadowed in a carving of the first century AD from the Russian Buddhist monastery at Airtam near Termez. This is now in the Hermitage Museum, Leningrad.

Juan Ruiz (*c.*1280–*c.*1350), Archpriest of Hita, spoke in his *Libro de Buen Amor* of the 'guitarra morisca' and 'guitarra latina', instruments which are both known to have been played at the court of the Duke of Normandy in 1349. The **guitarra morisca** is thought by some authorities to have been a long-necked instrument with oval-shaped body and vaulted back, while others believe that it was the mandora. The **guitarra latina**, which is generally known by the name **gittern**, resembled the Airtam carving in its approximately parallel sides, and normally had a flat back. (All three types are among the illustrations to the *Cantigas de Santa Maria* manuscript made in the late thirteenth century for King Alfonso X 'The Wise' of Castile, and now kept in the Escorial Library.) One of the most popular shapes resembled a holly leaf (Plate 11), while another was more curved at the lower end and had pointed 'wings' at the upper end of the body, causing Emanuel Winternitz to include it among the instruments derived from the kithara.

22.   Mandolin by Antoni Vinaccia, Naples, 1772. *London, Victoria and Albert Museum.*

23. Gittern, on a roof boss in the mid 14th-century Angel Choir of *Gloucester Cathedral*.

The neck was normally fretted, sometimes extending backwards to contain a hole for the left thumb, as can be seen in the surviving early fourteenth-century English gittern formerly in Warwick Castle and now in the British Museum. The gut strings were plucked with a plectrum, but their mediaeval tuning is not known to have been recorded; it is possible that they were tuned in the same way as the early lutes. The gittern was much used for singing and dancing, and in pictures is frequently seen to be played with a fiddle (Plate 180). During the fourteenth century it gradually gave way to the lute, being out of fashion, although still extant, after 1400.

By the mid fifteenth century there had emerged a new form of guitar known as **vihuela de mano** in Spain and **viola da mano** in Italy (Plate 42). With six courses of strings tuned like those of the lute, it was plucked in the new manner, with the fingers. (A guitar still plucked with a plectrum was described in Spain as a **vihuela de peñola**.) Tinctoris, who worked in Naples, said that 'while some play every sort of composition most delightfully on the lute, in Italy and Spain the viola without a bow is more often used'. For such an instrument Luis Milán published his instruction book *El Maestro* at Valencia in 1535/6, and a surviving example from this period can be seen in the Musée Jacquemart-André, Paris.

After Henry VIII died in 1547 an inventory of his instruments included

Foure Gitterons with iiii cases to them: they are caulled Spanishe Vialles.

It is uncertain whether these were the vihuela type mentioned above, or the new 'Gyttern' which, according to the Autobiography of Thomas Whythorne

(1528–96), was 'stranʒ in England, and þerfor þe more dezired and esteemed' when he stayed in London at the age of 17. This simpler form of instrument, with a smoother outline than its mediaeval ancestor and with somewhat incurved sides, had four single strings or double courses, and music for it appears in the *Mulliner Book* of *c.*1560. Praetorius called it 'Quinterna' and said that it could be tuned to *c f a d'* or *f b ♭ d' g'*. Following the tradition of the mediaeval gittern, its use as an instrument to provide rhythmical drones is brought to life by the character Dobinet Doughtie in Nicholas Udall's play *Royster Doyster*, written before 1553:

> Anon to our gitterne, thrumpledum, thrumpledum, thrumpledum thrum,
> Thrumpledum, thrumpledum, thrumpledum, thrumpledum thrum.

By the late sixteenth century the guitar had acquired a fifth course below the others and become known as the **Spanish Guitar**, being described in this form in Juan Carlos Amat's book *Guitarra Española de Cince Ordenes* which appeared at Gerona in 1639. Much music was published for the instrument in Italy, where '*Ziarlatini* and *Salt'inbanco* (who are like our comedians and buffoons) strum on them in singing their *Villanellen* and other foolish songs', to quote Praetorius. The Italian actor Francesco Corbetta was largely responsible for its popularity at the French court of Louis XIV after *c.*1655, and from there it spread to the England of Charles II who, according to Pepys's diary of 8 June 1660, brought a 'gittar' with him at the time of the Restoration. From this period there survive many guitars of fine workmanship by the best instrument makers of the day,

26. (Above) Guitar, in *The Music Lesson* painted by Edouard Manet (1832–83). *Boston, Mass., Museum of Fine Arts.*

24. (Left) *The Guitar Player* by Jacob van Schuppen (1670–1751). *Liverpool, Walker Art Gallery.*

25. (Below) Chitarra battente by Giorgio Sellas, Venice, 1627. *Oxford, Ashmolean Museum.*

leading to those of Antonio Stradivari of Cremona and Joachim Tielke of Hamburg. Some of these instruments had slightly vaulted backs, but in the **chitarra battente**, an Italian variant, this characteristic was normal; its chief difference from the regular instrument was in having metal strings plucked with a plectrum.

Shortly before and after 1800, several changes occurred. The shape of the guitar, which had been narrow and deep, became wider and shallower, and with greater incurving of the sides. The belly, which had been supported below by parallel bars, was now given fan-shaped barring, with considerable benefit to the sound, and its carved rose was omitted from the soundhole. The string courses became single and a sixth one was added, while the tuning was established at its present *E A d g b e'*. The fingerboard was lengthened to enable the performance of higher notes, and the pegs, which had previously been inserted from behind the pegbox, were replaced by machine pegs fitted at the side.

A Spanish guitar revival was brought about by the Cistercian Don Basilio (Miguel García) in the late eighteenth century, resulting in a flood of compositions by such composers as Fernando Sor (1778–1839) and Mauro Giuliani (1781–1829) who recognized the need for a more powerful and sonorous instrument. This became established in the mid nineteenth century, largely due to Antonio Torres (1817–92), who built the larger instrument still in use today. He also deepened the fingerboard, and widened it to cope more easily with the six strings, providing the model on which modern technique was founded by Francisco Tárrega (1852–1909). The great interest in the guitar today, together with numerous solo pieces and concertos which continually enlarge its repertoire, is largely due to the self-taught Andres Segovia, whose musicianship and virtuosity have inspired his disciples around the world.

The cittern family resembled that of the guitar in having a flat back, but differed in the tapering outline of its body, and in its metal strings. The mediaeval **citole** is thought to have been one of its forerunners, but convincing illustrations of such an instrument are hard to find. Since this book first went to press, Laurence Wright's article 'The Medieval Gittern and Citole: A case of mistaken identity' has appeared in the *Galpin Society Journal* XXX, 1977, 8–42. His suggestion that the above-mentioned mediaeval 'gittern' and 'mandora' should be called 'citole' and 'gittern' respectively, calls into question a long-accepted terminology, and poses a problem which may not immediately be solved.

An early example of the Renaissance **cittern** seems to have been the 'cetula' described by Tinctoris as having four brass or steel strings and 'only used in Italy by rustics to accompany light songs and lead dance music'. From the next two centuries many citterns survive. Praetorius enumerated several different types, from that 'with four courses of strings . . . a rather ignoble instrument played by cobblers and gardeners' ('Italian' if tuned to *b g d' e'* and 'French' if tuned to *a g d' e'*), to the cittern with 12 courses, which was 'almost as long as a bass viola da gamba' and 'produces a strong and magnificent sound like a harpsichord'; this was the archcittern, tuned to *eb Bb f c g d a e b g d' e'*. Mersenne said that the Italian citterns had fixed frets crossing the complete width of the fingerboard, while on French ones certain frets were set only below the top string. This, however, was not a fixed rule.

27. Cittern with the 'French' arrangement of frets. Detail from the German MS. *Splendor Solis*, 1582. *London, British Library, MS. Harl.3469, f.3.*

28. (Below) Orpharion from the title page of William Barley's *A nevv Booke of Tabliture for the Orpharion*, 1596. *London, British Library, MS. K.1.c.18.*

29. (Far below) English guitar by John Preston, London, *c.*1770. *London, Royal College of Music.*

30. (Left) Lyre-guitar by F. Roudhloff Mauchand, Paris, early 19th-century;
(Centre) Harp-guitar, English, early 19th-century; (Right) Dital harp by
Edward Light, London, c.1816. *London, Royal College of Music.*

Larger instruments of the cittern family included the **bandore**, apparently
invented by John Rose of London in 1562, and the **orpharion**, which was tuned
like a lute but had metal strings. Its stringholder was fixed onto the belly at a
slanted angle, in order to give the lowest strings the longest possible sounding
length. Further types included the **penorcon**, the **polyphant**, the bell-shaped
cittern known as **Hamburger Cithrinchen** which is particularly associated with
Joachim Tielke, and the eighteenth-century **English guitar**, a large cittern with
deep sides and six double courses tuned to $c\,e\,g\,c'\,e'\,g'$. In 1783 Christian Claus
produced citterns and guitars played by means of a small keyboard, but this
turned out to be a passing whim.

Around 1800 there appeared various hybrid types which combined characteristics of the lyre, harp, lute and guitar. Being decorous in appearance and easily
portable, they were popular for amateur music-making and for decorating the
studios of artists, but they did not find a place in the permanent musical repertoire.

— CHAPTER II —

Stringed Instruments – Bowed

While the plucking of strings fades into the mist of Antiquity, bowing is a comparatively recent invention. Werner Bachmann has suggested that it originated in Central Asia, around the River Oxus (Amu-Darya) in about the ninth century AD. This part of the world produced very fine hunting bows, and it may be that one of these was eventually brushed against the strings of a hitherto plucked instrument, creating a new sound. The discovery spread in all directions, being well documented soon after 900 in the lands of the Islamic and Byzantine Empires, where bowed instruments known respectively as *rabāb* and *lūrā* have been played ever since. (The Moroccan *rabāb* of today is often narrow in shape, with a right-angled pegbox and two strings, while the modern Greek *lyra* is wider, with a pegbox extending from the neck in the same plane, and three strings. Both instruments have a vaulted back.) Pictorial sources show that the bow had arrived in Spain and southern Italy in the tenth century, and by the early eleventh it had reached northern Europe.

Bowed instruments of mediaeval Europe were of many shapes and sizes, and their tuning was not standardized. They can, however, be broadly divided into the types of the rebec, crowd, mediaeval viol and fiddle, although generically the word 'fiddle' covers them all. (In this book the word is used in its particular sense.) The chief unifying factor is the bow, which varied in shape from being very arched to quite straight, and which, from early in its history, was strung with horsehair. It should be added here that there is a great deal of pictorial evidence for the bowing of instruments which were normally plucked, and vice versa, when certain sound effects were required.

The **rebec** family, which had reached England by 1050, had a vaulted back carved from one piece of wood, and its neck was formed by the gradual tapering of the body. It included both the *rabāb* and *lūrā* types, presumably accounting for the Latin names *rubeba* and *lira* which were often used in the Middle Ages, as were variants of the word *gigue*. From c.1300 the word *rebec* appears, coinciding with the development of a sickle-shaped pegbox which eventually led to that of the violin. The Dominican friar Jerome of Moravia (d.1304), in his *Tractatus de Musica* written in Paris after 1272, said that the 'rubeba', which was held 'close to its head', was tuned to *c* and *g*. The number of strings, however, varied from one to about five, and sometimes they were tuned in pairs. When, as often, there

43

31.   Rebec, played by one of David's minstrels, while another juggles with knives. Detail from an MS. of St Augustine's *Commentary on the Psalms* (1–50), written *c*.1070–1100 at Christ Church, Canterbury, by monks brought from the Norman abbey of Bec by Archbishop Lanfranc. *Cambridge, Trinity College, MS. B.5.26, f.1.*

was a flat bridge, allowing for drones around a melody, the strings could have been tuned in fifths and fourths, as were those of certain fiddles (see p. 50). In 1545 Martin Agricola, in his *Musica Instrumentalis Deudsch* (originally published at Wittemberg in 1528), gave the following tunings: treble g d' a'; alto and tenor c g d'; bass F G d a. Although he said that these 'kleine Geigen one bünde' generally had no frets, he was only describing the average rebecs, and many pictures do show them fretted. In England the playing position was up at the shoulder (even if pointing downwards) or at the chest, but on the Continent it was sometimes down on the lap. The rebec, which was often played for dancing, lasted beyond the mediaeval period, and eventually merged with the kit (see p. 68).

When the bow arrived in northern Europe it was very soon applied to different forms of lyre, particularly that which had a central neck running from the yoke to the soundbox. The resulting instrument, known as **crowde** or **crouthe** in England, had about four strings over the neck and sometimes two lateral drones. As the Welsh **crwth** this type was played as accompaniment to the voice in ceremonies of the bards, and survived into the twentieth century. No mediaeval tunings for it are known, but in the eighteenth century both Daines Barrington in *Archaeologia* iii (1775) and Edward Jones in *Musical and Poetical Relicks of the*

32. Rebec with three main strings and a lateral drone, played with singers in the initial C(antate Domino). Detail from an English Psalter, *c.*1250–75. *Venice, Biblioteca Nazionale Marciana, MS. Lat.I.77, f.115.*

33. Rebec with frets, played by an angel in *The Virgin and Child with Musical Angels* (*c.*1500) by the anonymous Flemish artist, the Master of the Morrisson Triptych. *Brussels, Musées Royaux des Beaux Arts.*

Welsh Bards (London, 1784) gave g g' / c' c'' d' d'', to be followed soon afterwards by a a' / e' e'' b' b'' recorded by William Bingley in *North Wales* ii (London, 1804). (Canon Galpin has suggested that this last tuning was intended to be an octave lower.) Each upper pair of strings was to be bowed together, the lower string in each case droning an accompaniment to the melody, while the two lateral drones (the first two notes listed in each tuning) could be plucked by the left thumb or touched with the bow. That the crowder played at least two notes at once during the Middle Ages is evident from the commentary on Psalm 150 by Richard Rolle of Hampole (*c.*1340) who renders 'in choro' as 'in croude, that is, in pesful felagheship and concorde of voicys . . .'. The Latin word *chorus* was frequently used for the bowed lyre in England at this time, and is listed as such in the *Promptorium Parvulorum* of *c.*1440: 'Crowde, instrument of musyke.   *Chorus.*'

34. (Right) Bowed lyre, held by David in a 12th-century French ivory carving on the cover of the *Lothair Psalter. London, British Library, MS. Add. 37768.*

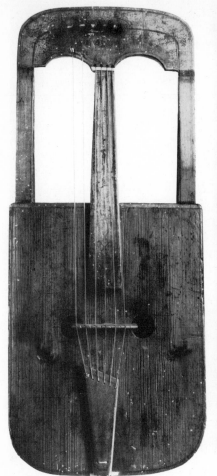

35.   (Left) Crwth by Richard Evans, 1742. *Cardiff, Welsh Folk Museum, St Fagan's Castle.*

36.   (Right) Two crowdes played by angels in feathered costumes such as were worn in dramatic performances. Detail from stained glass windows made by John Prudde in 1447. *Warwick, St Mary's Church, Beauchamp Chapel.*

The **mediaeval viol** answered the need for a large instrument which could produce lower notes than those of the rebec of its time. The performer was usually seated, holding the viol down in his lap and gripping the bow from beneath. The shape of the instrument varied from being almost oval to like a figure of eight, often having some indentation of the sides; the pegbox was flat, and the strings generally numbered from three to five; the author has found no evidence of frets. No special name seems to have been used for this type of instrument, so it must have been covered by the Latin *viella* and *viola* and the various forms of *fiddle*

37. Mediaeval viol of a typical shape, although incorrectly fingered by the performer. Detail from a 13th-century Psalter illustrated in England by William de Brailes. *Cambridge, Fitzwilliam Museum, MS. 330, leaf 5.*

which appear in different languages of the period. European art shows it to have been flourishing during the twelfth and thirteenth centuries, but traceable back to the tenth in Spain; after 1300 it gradually disappeared.

Mediaeval minstrels often walked around as they played, for instance in processions or dances, and for this the mediaeval viol was unsuitable. The answer to the problem came with the instrument which has become known in the specific sense as the **mediaeval fiddle**. This fiddle (**fedyll, fiedel, fyþele, viella, vielle, viola, vihuela de arco,** etc.), which was generally held in the same positions as the rebec, could be found in numerous shapes and sizes, but its chief characteristics were *either* (a) a flat back, *or* (b) a neck which was distinct from the body even if carved

38. Fiddle with five strings, including a lateral drone, in the Angel Choir (before 1280) of *Lincoln Cathedral.*

from the same piece of wood. The best kind of fiddle combined these ingredients, and can be seen in a carving at Lincoln Cathedral (Plate 38), which also shows the prevalent flat-topped pegbox and a lateral drone besides four strings over the neck. This example is almost contemporary with Jerome of Moravia's three tunings for the 'viella', the first of which had just such a string formation:

a) $d/Ggd'd'$ b) $Gdgd'g'$ c) $GGdc'c'$.

His second tuning is one which could be used to good effect on an instrument with a flat bridge, when all the strings were played together for permanent droning. Tinctoris, writing in the 1480s, also described the tuning of fifths and unisons for a fiddle ('viola') with five strings, but said that one with three strings was tuned in fifths. He pointed out that at that time the bridge was generally curved so that the bow could touch one string alone, a necessity for the polyphonic instrumental music of the age. Many pictures show a combined bridge and tailpiece, thereby allowing a longer sounding length (and consequently deeper notes) than if they were separate. Although the fiddle was depicted in Byzantine manuscripts of the eleventh century, it only became widespread in northern Europe c.1200, and from c.1300 onwards it is sometimes shown to have frets. That it was one of the most

39.   Fiddle showing overlapping edges and a wedge between the neck and
fingerboard; both characteristics were later to be found on early violins.
Detail from *The Coronation of the Virgin* by the anonymous German artist,
the Master of the Life of Mary (*fl.* 1460–80). *Munich, Alte Pinakothek.*

versatile of mediaeval instruments was indicated by Joannes de Grocheo in his
treatise *De Musica* (*c.*1300) where he said:

... thus does the fiddle ['viella'] include within itself all other instruments. ...
A good artist plays on the fiddle every *cantus* and *cantilena* and every musical
form in general.

This implies that the fiddler could play in many different styles and must therefore have known about slurred bowing, a point which has until recently been disputed. Grocheo adds that at feasts it was used for the performance of songs and dances. Tinctoris, besides saying that the fiddle ('viola cum arculo') was used in the recitation of epics, describes

> A recent event, the performance of two Flemings, the brothers Charles and Jean Orbus, who are no less learned in letters than skilled in music. At Bruges, I heard Charles take the treble and Jean the tenor in many songs, playing this kind of fiddle so expertly and with such charm that the fiddle has never pleased me so well.

While England was using the mediaeval-type fiddle until well into the reign of Henry VIII, Renaissance Italy had already produced two developments from it. These were the **lira da braccio** and the **viola da braccio,** both of which were played at the shoulder or chest. The first represents the culmination of the Lincoln-type fiddle (Plate 38), the chief differences between them being that (a) the lira da braccio generally had five strings over the fingerboard and two lateral drones, tuned according to the relative pitch of Giovanni Maria Lanfranco (*Scintille di Musica*, Brescia, 1533) at *d d' / g g' d' a' e''*, and according to Praetorius (1619) at

40.   Lira da braccio and lute. Detail from *The Virgin and Saints* by Giambattista Cima da Conegliano (*c.*1459–1517/18). *Venice, Galleria dell'Accademia.*

$dd'/gg'd'a'd''$; (b) the sides were often, but not invariably, more indented; (c) the back and sides of the instrument were now regularly made from separate pieces of wood, a technical advance which is shown in certain pictures of fiddles from the fourteenth century onwards. The bridge was only slightly curved, allowing the performer to play several strings at once if he wanted to. Singing to one's own accompaniment on the lira da braccio was regarded, in Renaissance Italy, as being one of the best ways of making music. A larger and deeper-sounding instrument of the same family, which emerged somewhat later, was the **lira da gamba** or **lirone**, which had many strings and was played between the knees or on the lap.

The name *viola da braccio* was used in Italy in a general sense to cover most bowed instruments played up at the shoulder or across the arm (as opposed to those held *a gamba*, at the legs), so it was sometimes applied to the lira da braccio and also to members of the violin family. There was, however, another type of instrument to which the name is now given in the more specific sense. This was derived from that type of mediaeval fiddle which had no lateral drone strings. Its sides were deep and with pronounced bouts, the soundholes were often c-shaped, and the strings numbered about four. The pegbox could be flat or ending in a scroll, and there seems to have been no fixed rule about frets. Pictures show it being played for dances and feasts, and in scenes from mythology.

41. Lira da gamba played by the *Homer* of Pier Francesco Mola (1612–68). *Dresden, Gemäldegalerie.*

While these instruments were leading to the appearance of the violin, a new **viol** had emerged in southern Europe (probably in Spain) in the latter half of the fifteenth century. It was held *a gamba* like its mediaeval predecessor, but was now furnished with gut frets, which by that time were also seen frequently on fiddles. At first this type of instrument had no standardization of shape or tuning, but by the time that Sylvestro Ganassi's *Regola Rubertina* was published at Venice in 1542/3, certain sizes were played together regularly in consort. Ganassi gave what became the traditional (but not inflexible) tuning for their six strings as: **discant** *d g c′ e′ a′ d″*; **alto** and **tenor** *G c f a d′ g′*; **bass** *D G c e a d′*. He also mentioned types with three or four strings. The viol was characterized by deep sides and a flat back sloping inwards at the upper end, while the belly, which was slightly curved, contained two soundholes, either *c* or *f*-shaped, and sometimes also a carved rose. The neck ended in a sickle-shaped pegbox surmounted by a scroll or carved head in most cases, although some early pictures show the pegbox to be flat or at a right angle.

While there is a good deal of evidence as to the use of viols on the Continent in the late fifteenth century, they apparently did not become established in England until the reign of Henry VIII. The earliest known viol players at his court had Flemish names, such as Matthew de Weldre, a player of lutes and 'veoldes' in

42.   Bass viol, viola da braccio, viola da mano, rebec and bass viol; one of four groups of musical angels from the wall-painting *The Coronation of the Virgin* attributed to either Ludovico Mazzolino or Michele Coltellini, *c*.1510. *Ferrara, Church of Santa Maria della Consolazione.*

43.   Tenor viol from *The Virgin and Child with Angels* by the Spanish painter Rodrigo de Orsuna II, *c.*1510. *Barcelona, Museum of Catalan Art.*

1517, and they were soon joined by musicians from northern Italy. When the king died in 1547 he owned 25 viols 'greate and small', and by that time other noble families, such as those of the earls of Rutland and Exeter, also had collections. The instrument which had arrived so late in England was then cultivated to such an extent that its makers there, such as John Rose, Henry Jaye and Barak Norman were among the best in Europe. The London lawyer Roger North (*c*.1651–1734), writing about music in seventeenth-century England, said that a 'chest of viols' (consisting of two trebles, two 'means' and two basses) 'seldome wanted in a musicall family'. His reference to the '*Respublica* of Consort' shows how the viols of different sizes were equally important during the Golden Age of polyphony:

> The violls bore all an equall share in the consort, and carrying the same aire, there was no reason to choose one part before another.

The consort of viols reached its culmination in the fantasias of Henry Purcell (1680), but it was then already giving way to the violin family. The bass viol, however, stayed in use for some time as a continuo instrument, and was occasionally given a special *obbligato* part such as in 'Komm, süsses Kreuz' from Bach's *St Matthew Passion*. Yet even in the age of consorts the bass viol had been used as a virtuoso instrument, its complexity being shown already by Diego Ortiz in *Tratado de Glosas* (Rome, 1553) and later by Christopher Simpson in *The Division Viol* (London, 1667). Divisions in this case were variations upon a ground bass, and to facilitate the technical problems involved, the instrument on which they were played was usually slightly smaller than a consort bass. So also was the **lyra viol**, which flourished during the seventeenth century and had many tunings (sometimes with sympathetic strings) to suit its music, most of which was written in tablature. This instrument, of all the viols, came closest to playing complete polyphony on its own. Among its outstanding performers was the composer John Jenkins, who, according to North,

> once was brought to play upon the lyra viol afore King Charles I, as one that performed somewhat extraordinary; and after he had done the King sayd he did wonders upon an inconsiderable instrument.

The **double bass viol**, known in Italy as **violone** (this word was also used for other large viols and for the double bass of the violins) was already in use in the sixteenth century but continued to be played long after the smaller members of the family had gone out of fashion. With six strings tuned about a fifth below those of the consort bass, it was played when needed in viol consorts, or as a continuo instrument, eventually merging with the violin family's double bass.

The smallest viol appeared late on the scene. Known as **pardessus de viole**, it emerged in France during the latter part of the seventeenth century, and was used mainly by ladies of the French court. It was smaller than the treble viol and tuned a fourth higher, and its repertoire consisted to a great extent of variations on popular tunes.

44. Division viol by Barak Norman, London, 1692. *London, Royal College of Music.*

When Jenkins played to Charles I he was using an instrument of noble traditions which, according to the *Epitome Musicale* (Lyon, 1556) of the Frenchman Philibert Jambe de Fer, was played by 'gentlemen, merchants and other virtuous people'. The **violin family**, however, had, in the words of North, 'bin little in England except by comon fidlers' until the reign of Charles II. This monarch, who came to the throne in 1660, 'set up a band of twenty-four violins to play at his dinners, which disbanded all the old English music at once'. Being brighter in sound than the viols, the violin family was better suited to the new Italian-type music which needed instruments capable of standing out in contrast to others, and yet blending when necessary. In appearance the violin had, and still has, shallower sides than the viols, its soundboard and back are both slightly curved with overlapping edges, and its soundholes are *f*-shaped. The neck, with its unfretted fingerboard, ends in a pegbox surmounted by a scroll, while the four strings pass over a curved bridge before being attached to a tailpiece at the lower end. The usual tunings for the smaller instruments of this family are now: **violin** *g d' a' e''*; **viola** *c g d' a'*; **cello** *C G d a*, but the cello in its early days was larger, being called the **bass violin** and sometimes being tuned to *Bb' F c g*. The intermediate **tenor violin** (see plates 136 and 193) flourished from the sixteenth to eighteenth centuries, and was tuned about half-way between the viola and bass violin. It may have been the instrument to which Burney referred, when, writing about the Bohemian musician Francis Benda, he said that 'early in his life . . . he was remembered to play the tenor, in the concerts performed by the singing boys at Dresden'. (It should be mentioned, however, that the expression 'tenor violin' has also been applied to the viola.) From the sixteenth to the eighteenth centuries there existed also a **violino piccolo**, tuned higher than the normal violin; its bottom string was sometimes *c'*, but Bach set it at *bb* in his *First Brandenburg Concerto* (1721). Another short-lived instrument of the family was the **viola pomposa** or **violino pomposo** which had five strings, those of the ordinary viola with the addition of the violin *e''*; its repertoire dates mainly from the eighteenth century. *Scordatura*, the tuning of strings at unusual intervals to facilitate double stopping, has always been a possibility, one of the chief composers to make use of it being the German, Heinrich Biber (1644–1704).

45. Violin, from a wall painting by Garofalo, 1505–1508. *Ferrara, Palazzo di Ludovico il Moro, Sala del Tesoro.*

The earliest violins were until recently thought to date from the 1520s, but now earlier sources have come to light, among them a painting by Garofalo or his assistants at the Palazzo di Ludovico il Moro at Ferrara in 1505–8. In 1535–6 Gaudenzio Ferrari painted the cupola of the Santuario at Saronno, showing numerous musical angels, two of which play a violin and viola; another instrument, apparently a small bass or large tenor, has frets. Four strings had become established by 1556 when Jambe de Fer described the instruments and gave the modern tunings for the violin and viola.

One of the earliest known violin-makers was Andrea Amati of Cremona, who was born not later than 1511. Two three-string violins made by him in 1542 and 1546 were said to be in existence during the nineteenth century, but both have now disappeared. One dated 1564, now in the Ashmolean Museum at Oxford, is from a collection of violins, violas and basses which he was commissioned to make for Charles IX of France. This instrument represents the fully-fledged violin with four strings, which was brought to perfection by his grandson Nicola Amati (1596–1684) and the latter's disciple Antonio Stradivari (1644–1737), known as Stradivarius. The Amati violins were characterized by considerable arching of the soundboard, as were those of Jakob Stainer (1621–83) of Absam near Innsbruck, for many years the chief violin maker outside Italy. In contrast to this, Brescia, which had long been a centre for expert instrument-making, produced much flatter models, made at first by Gasparo da Salò (Gasparo Bertolotti, 1540–1609) and his pupil Giovanni Paolo Maggini (1580–c.1632). Stradivarius, after making his earlier instruments in the style of the Amati, finally settled for a smoother shape in his 'classical' model, as exemplified by the celebrated 'Messiah' violin (1716) which is now in the Ashmolean Museum, Oxford.

In the lifetime of Andrea Amati, instruments of the violin family were used mainly to double voices or other instruments, and were played particularly for dancing. No solo music has survived for them from that period. By the early seventeenth century, however, special pieces were being written with the violin in mind, although they could also be played on other instruments. Some of the works by Giovanni Battista Fontana (d.1630) and Biagio Marini (1597–1665), for instance, were for 'violin or cornett' and continuo. The pursuit of a violinistic idiom and the consequent development of technique were furthered to a great extent at Modena, Bologna, Venice and Rome, coinciding with the lives of Stradivarius and his contemporary Giuseppe Guarneri (del Gesù) of the Guarnerius family.

By the late eighteenth century, conditions of performance had changed so much that the instruments needed to be altered. This was partly due to the need for a stronger and more penetrating sound, particularly when a soloist was playing a concerto in a large hall and had to hold his own against an orchestra. To contribute to this sound, the performance pitch was raised and the strings tightened. The consequent increase in tension demanded the strengthening of the bridge, together with that of the soundpost and bassbar, through which it transmitted vibrations to the back and belly respectively. Other alterations involved the neck and fingerboard. As early as 1715, Vivaldi's 'fingers almost touched the bridge, so that there was hardly any room left for the bow', according to the diary of Johann Friedrich Uffenbach. It was necessary, therefore, for the fingerboard and neck to be lengthened. In its existing position the neck was built to continue on the same plane as the belly, and the fingerboard was tilted into a suitable playing position by an intermediary wedge. The wedge was now removed and the fingerboard made to rest directly on the neck, which itself was tilted at an oblique angle. The removal of the wedge enabled the performer to climb more easily into the higher positions than before. These changes were accomplished just before the appearance on the scene of the supreme Italian violinist Nicolò Paganini (1782–1840). Since that time no great structural changes have taken place in the violin itself, but the addition of the chinrest by Louis Spohr c.1820 gave the performer a better grip on the instrument, thereby allowing more freedom of movement to the left arm.

Although the violin, viola, tenor and bass violins and double bass were all in existence during the sixteenth century, the treble violin was for a long time the most important member of the family, the others being used mainly for supporting roles. The reduction in size of the bass violin (which was sometimes called *violone*) to become the violoncello was reflected in the instruments made during the long lifetime of Stradivarius, and made possible more refined and difficult music than before, such as the cello concertos of Vivaldi and the solo sonatas of Bach. (Some of the earliest known pieces for solo cello had been written by Domenico Gabrielli in 1689.) The viola, with ribs shallow in proportion to the depth of its sound, had

46. (Overleaf) Three different sizes of the violin family, together with a lute, cymbals and hybrid fiddle, painted by Gaudenzio Ferrari in 1535–6. *Saronno, Church of Santa Maria dei Miracoli (Il Santuario).*

a small tone, and at first was given little consideration by composers; its music only began to acquire real independence with the flowering of the string quartet in the mid eighteenth century. Mozart's *Sinfonia Concertante* for violin and viola, one of the earliest concertos for the latter instrument, called for it to be tuned a semitone higher than usual in order to produce a brighter sound. In spite of Berlioz's *Harold in Italy* (1834), a 'symphony with viola solo' written originally for Paganini, the viola's repertoire increased only gradually during the nineteenth century, and there were few good players. Only in the last 50 years has its recognition been consolidated, largely due to the efforts of Paul Hindemith, William Primrose and Lionel Tertis, who designed a larger and more powerful instrument.

The **double bass**, making a harsher sound than the violone of the viol family, was for a time used for less distinguished music. Around 1800, however, the two merged, the general shape of the violone being preserved, but with fewer strings and no frets. Even so, the instrument did not become standardized like the higher members of its family. Its shape can resemble a violin or viol, and its strings have varied in number between three and five, although today the most usual number is four, tuned to $EAdg$, and sounding an octave lower. Just as the altered violin appeared in time for Paganini, so the adapted double bass was ready for the virtuoso Domenico Dragonetti (1763–1846), whose reputation was such that he could command the same fees as the best singers of his day. Until this time the bow had been held with the palm uppermost, as with the viols, but it was another Italian virtuoso, Giovanni Bottesini (1822–89) who introduced the violin manner of bowing (with the palm facing downwards) to the double bass. Since his time, both techniques have continued to be used.

Besides the instruments themselves, the strings and bow have also undergone changes. At first gut strings were normal, but the thickness of the lowest one produced an inadequate tone, and composers avoided it when they could, particularly in solo music. This problem was resolved by the lowest strings for each instrument being wound round with wire, an invention attributed in Jean Rousseau's *Traité de la Viole* (Paris, 1687) to the Sieur de Sainte-Colombe around 1675. The frequent breaking of the violin gut e'' led to its being made of wire from early in the twentieth century. Nowadays strings for all bowed instruments can be obtained in very varying materials, ranging from nylon to wire covered by aluminium or silver.

The **bow** or *fydylstyk* of the Middle Ages varied from being quite straight to very curved, depending to a great extent on the shape of the instrument's bridge and on the type of music to be played. Its hairs were generally knotted or glued at each end. Many Renaissance pictures show at the heel a knob which might possibly represent some form of screw, but is perhaps more likely to have been a covering for an otherwise untidy end. Often the hairs are supported in position by a nut or frog, which could be of one piece with the bow stick or else detachable so that the hairs could be loosened. During the seventeenth century the tension was

47. (Left) Violin, made by Andrea Amati of Cremona for Charles IX of France, in 1574. *Carlisle Museum and Art Gallery.*

48. Cello, harpsichord and mandora played together in *Frederick, Prince of Wales, and his sisters,* by Philip Mercier, 1733. *London, National Portrait Gallery.*

49. Double bass, made in Italy in the 17th century; this extra-large specimen was once owned by Dragonetti. *London, Victoria and Albert Museum.*

sometimes regulated by a series of notches, but by 1700 its smooth and gradual alteration by means of a screw was well established. The Renaissance and Baroque bows were generally convex and with a carefully tapered point which was well suited to the musical style of the time. With the need for a more powerful sound, the bow gradually became longer and concave in shape and swelled out towards the point, this form being perfected *c.*1780 by François Tourte in France and John Dodd in England, and still in use today. Viola bows are longer than those of the violin, but cello and double bass ones are shorter and heavier, the latter type varying in shape according to whether it is played with the palm of the hand facing up or down.

Since 1964 a new family of violins has been developed by Mrs Carleen Hutchins and others of the Catgut Acoustical Society of America. Built in the proportions of the actual violin, and with particular attention to acoustical values, there are eight different sizes, ranging from 'large bass' (bottom string *E'*) to 'treble' (top

50.   The New Violin Family (its contrabass is 8′ long) made by Carleen Hutchins of Montclair, New Jersey.

string *e'''*). Played together they produce a full and homogenous sound hitherto unknown, and special works have been commissioned for them.

Two instruments of the seventeenth and eighteenth centuries combined characteristics of the viol and violin families. These were the **baryton** and the **viola d'amore**, both of which were widely played, although not as regular members of consorts and orchestras except in special circumstances.

The baryton somewhat resembled a bass viol in size and shape, but was distinguished by a row of wire sympathetic strings, arranged in such a way that they could be plucked from behind by the left thumb. The instrument was normally unfretted, an exception being the baryton by Magnus Feldlen, dated 1647, which is now at the Royal College of Music, London. The instrument's chief extant repertoire, however, was written over 100 years later by Joseph Haydn for that enthusiastic performer Prince Nicholas Esterhazy.

The viola d'amore was played at the shoulder like the violin, and was also

51. Baryton by Magnus Feldlen, Vienna, 1647. *London, Royal College of Music.*

52.   Viola d'amore by Jean Nicolas Lambert, Paris, 1772. *London, Victoria and Albert Museum.*

54.   (Above right) Kit by a 17th-century Italian maker. *London, Royal College of Music.*

53.   (Right) Kit by Antonio Stradivari, 1717. *Paris, Conservatoire National Supérieur de Musique.*

unfretted. Its six or seven gut and covered melody strings were doubled by sympathetic strings of steel below the fingerboard, and a form of the instrument with 14 sympathetic strings was described by Leopold Mozart, in his *Treatise on the Fundamental Principles of Violin Playing* (1756) as the 'English violet'. To allow for elaborate double stopping there were numerous *scordatura* tunings. Leopold Mozart also wrote that the viola d'amore sounded 'especially charming in the stillness of the evening'. A related instrument which has survived until today as a folk instrument in Norway is the much decorated *Hardanger Fiddle*.

The smallest bowed instrument, and one of the most interesting on account of the diversity of its construction, is the **kit** or **pochette**. Emerging from the rebec in the sixteenth century, it first took the shape of a narrow boat (seen on the left of plate 191), and about 100 years later began to resemble viols, then violins, and eventually viole d'amore. (This last type, with its sympathetic strings, was known as the **pochette d'amour**.) It had a long unfretted neck, and was tuned about a fourth or fifth above the violin, or even an octave above when there were only three strings. Used to a great extent by dancing masters, it survived into the nineteenth century, and was used for a gavotte in the opera *Les Trois Nicolas* (1859) by Louis Clapisson, who had recently acquired a kit by Stradivarius. This instrument (plate 53) is now in the museum of the Paris Conservatoire, where Clapisson was the first curator.

55. Trumpet marine, in stained glass from the workshop of Peter Hemmel
von Andlau, Strassburg, late 15th century. *Basel, Historisches Museum.*

Unconnected in any great degree to the foregoing instruments was the **arpeggione**, a form of bowed guitar with metal frets, invented by Georg Staufer of Vienna in 1823. Although it was not given lasting recognition, its place in history has been assured by the sonata written for it in the following year by Schubert; this is nowadays played on the cello.

Of curious distinction is the **trumpet marine** (**tromba marina, Trumscheit**). Descended from a plucked form of monochord carved on a Romanesque capital in the abbey of Vézelay, it was bowed from the fifteenth century onwards, being played up at the shoulder or resting on the ground; at that time it had from one to four strings. These were touched lightly by the fingers or thumb of the left hand, sounding the notes of the harmonic series. A 'buzzing or snarling' (Praetorius) was produced, either by one foot of the bridge being free to vibrate against the soundboard, or by an extra piece of wood suitably placed for that purpose. Praetorius added that 'the trumpet marine sounds much more pleasant from a distance than when one listens to it close by'. It survived for several hundred years, acquiring a virtuoso in Jean Baptiste Prin (*c.*1650–1742) who added to a one-string instrument numerous sympathetic strings inside. In the *London Gazette* of 4–8 February 1674 there appeared the advertisement

A Rare Concert of four Trumpets Marine, never heard before in *England*. If any persons desire to come and hear it, they may repair to the Fleece Tavern, near St. Iames's, about two of the clock in the Afternoon every day in the Week (except Sundays). Every concert shall continue one hour, and so to begin again; the best places are one shilling, the other [sic] six pence.

This may have been the first public performance on such instruments in England, but Samuel Pepys had written in his diary for 24 October 1667

. . . we in to see a Frenchman . . . one Monsieur Prin, play on the Trump. Marine, which he doth beyond belief; and the truth is, it doth so far out-do a Trumpet as nothing more, and he doth play anything very true and it is most remarkable; and at first was a mystery to me that I should hear a whole consort of chords together at the end of a pause, but he showed me that it was only when the last notes were fifths or thirds one to another, and then their sounds like an Echo did last, so as they seemed to sound all together. The instrument is open at the end I discovered, but he would not let me look into it; but I was mightily pleased with it, and he did take great pains to show me all he could do on it, which was very much – and would make an excellent consort, two or three of them, better than trumpets can ever do because of their want of compass.

Perhaps the enthusiasm of Pepys led to the concerts in the Fleece Tavern nearly seven years later.

One of the strangest bowed instruments is the **nail violin**, said to have been invented by the court violinist Johann Wilde of St Petersburg *c.*1740, after noticing that a squeak occurred when he hung his bow up on a nail. He therefore devized a circular-headed soundbox on which were fixed nails of different sounding lengths and thicknesses, and these were duly bowed. The instrument was given sympathetic strings by Senal of Bohemia *c.*1780, and crept into the realms of art music by being included in special compositions, among them the *Quartet for Nail Violin, two Violins and Cello* by Friedrich Wilhelm Rust, dating from 1787.

56.   Trumpet marine, designed to contain sympathetic strings. (?) French, 18th century. *London, Victoria and Albert Museum.*

57.   (Below) Nail violin, early 19th century. *London, Royal College of Music.*

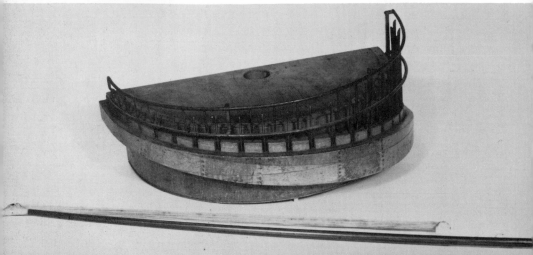

CHAPTER III

Stringed Instruments with Keyboards

The first stringed instrument to receive a keyboard mechanism was the **organistrum**, which was well established in Europe by the middle of the twelfth century. Built in a shape resembling that of a mediaeval viol, it was laid across the laps of two performers. One of them turned a handle which rotated a rosined wheel, and this itself rubbed against the strings, taking the place of a bow in producing the sound. The other player activated a set of revolvable rods which were each shaped at a certain point to form a bridge-like tangent. When a rod was turned, its tangent came into contact with all the strings at once, causing them to sound together. In the Romanesque period there were generally three strings, but our information on their tuning is scanty. A thirteenth-century manuscript from the

58. Organistrum, played by two Elders of the Apocalypse in the *Portico de la Gloria* (1188) of *Santiago de Compostela Cathedral*.

German monastery of St Blasien (reproduced in Martin Gerbert's *De Cantu et Musica Sacra* published there in 1774, but since destroyed) shows that from the open string to the top tangent the major scale of C could be played, plus the B♭ within its range. Unfortunately, the symbols which may represent the tunings of the other two strings have not yet been sufficiently elucidated. Bearing in mind that certain fiddles were tuned in fifths, fourths and octaves (see page   ), it is possible that such a tuning was also applied to the organistrum. With the mechanism described above, the melody would then have proceeded in the motion of parallel organum, a style which, although already old, was still sometimes used in singing.

The organistrum continued in use for a time after 1200, and then gradually gave way to a smaller version known as the **symphony**, which could be carried and played at once by one person. At about the same time the mechanism changed. Instead of twisting a rod which touched all the strings together, the performer pressed a key of which an inner part, forming a tangent, touched only the top string (*chanterelle*), while the others gave unstopped drones. This system, which

59. Symphony with chromatic keyboard, in the stained glass (1501/2) of the north transept at *Great Malvern Priory.*

60. (Right) Hurdy-gurdy by Pierre Louvet, Paris, mid 18th century. *London, Victoria and Albert Museum.*

allowed for much faster playing, was better suited to secular songs and dances than was the earlier one, and in these contexts the symphony was mentioned in numerous poems. One example is John Lydgate's *Pilgrimage of the Life of Man* (translated from the fourteenth-century French of Guillaume de Deguilleville), where Miss Idleness says

> I teche hem ek, (lyk ther ententys,)
> To pleye on sondry Instrumentys,
> On Harpe, lut, & on gyterne,
> And to revelle at taverne,
> Wyth al merthe & mellodye,
> On rebube and on symphonye . . .

It was, however, gradually losing prestige, as this poem indicates, and although by 1500 it had acquired two or three more strings and a chromatic keyboard, it became associated chiefly with wandering minstrels and with folk music.

In the eighteenth century, when the French nobility created for themselves a genteel rusticity, the existing **vielle à roue**, as it was called, returned to court. New ones were built, often of a magnificence unknown to the peasantry, while others were made from converted lutes and guitars. A frequent tuning arrangement consisted of

2 melody strings (*chanterelles*) tuned to g′ (with a compass of two octaves)
4 drone strings, i.e.

   Trompette (copper) tuned to c′ or d′

   Mouche (gut) tuned to g

   2 *Bourdons* (wire-covered) tuned to G and c, or G and d

and certain instruments were given sympathetic strings. In England the name of this instrument was **hurdy-gurdy**. Several hybrid types have appeared from time to time, one form using a bow instead of a wheel, as can still be seen in the Swedish *nyckelharpa*, while another version had the wheel but no keys, with the strings

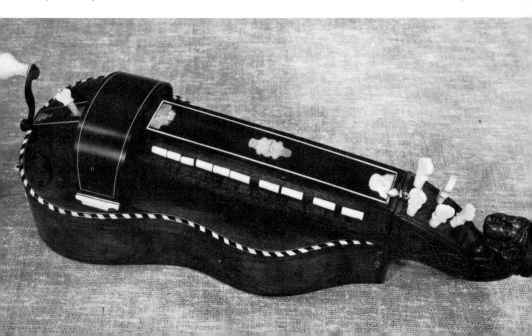

touched directly by the performer's fingers. In the eighteenth century the addition of organ pipes resulted in the **organ hurdy-gurdy** or **lira organizzata**, an instrument played by King Ferdinand IV of Naples for whom Haydn wrote five concertos. Today the hurdy-gurdy is a respected folk instrument in several countries, notably Hungary, the north of Spain, and the central part of France.

The next stringed keyboard instrument to appear was the **exchiquier** or **chekker**, which was already known in England in 1360, when Edward III gave one to John II of France; Guillaume de Machaut, in his poem *La Prise d'Alexandrie* (*c.*1367) emphasizes the English connection by his reference to 'l'eschaquier d'Engletere'. John I of Aragon's description of it in a letter to Juan de Montra (1388) as 'resembling an organ which sounds with strings' has led some authorities to believe that it may have been a clavicytherium (see page 80), but the Spanish king may only have been making his comparison over the keyboard. An account book of the French royal court for 1488 refers to the purchase of an 'eschiquier ou manichordion', the latter word generally being used at that time for a clavichord. On the basis of this and other evidence, Edwin M. Ripin in his article 'Towards an Identification of the Chekker' (*GSJ* XXVIII, 1975, 11–25) presented a case for the chekker being, after all, a clavichord.

The **clavichord** was a rectangular instrument with its strings running parallel to the keyboard. When a key was depressed, it levered up a brass tangent which struck a pair of strings from below and remained there until the performer's finger left the key. Thus the sound was sustained, although it was very quiet, due to the short distance which the tangent could travel; a vibrato (*Bebung*), however, could be obtained for expressive purposes.

The strings of the clavichord sounded only between the tangents and a bridge at the right-hand end of the instrument, as their other sections were dampened by felt at the left-hand end. Just as the pitch of the monochord could be adjusted by a movable bridge, so on the clavichord (which is really a collection of monochords) it was dependent on the placing of the tangents. The early clavichords were 'fretted', having more keys than strings. Most strings therefore had to be struck by two or more tangents, so care was taken to ensure that they produced notes which were not normally sounded together. At first all the strings were of equal length and tuned to the same note, with the tangents placed so as to produce about one diatonic octave. By about 1440, however, when Henricus Arnault of Zwolle wrote a treatise on the building of certain instruments (Paris, Bibliothèque Nationale MS Lat. 7295), the range had reached three chromatic octaves (*B* – *b″*), all obtainable from nine pairs of strings. The next step was to increase the number of strings, and to make them in different lengths and pitches, an advance which had taken place before 1500. The latest important development came in the eighteenth century with the appearance of unfretted clavichords, in which each key had its own pair of strings, and the range had reached five octaves. To suit the greater number of strings, the instruments were made larger and stronger than before, a notable example being that made for C.P.E. Bach by Gottfried Silbermann. In the words of the German composer Johann Friedrich Reichardt (*Briefe eines aufmerksamen Reisenden*, Frankfurt, 1774),

61.   Clavichord and harpsichord, played by angels in the stained glass by
John Prudde (1447) at *Warwick, St Mary's Church, Beauchamp Chapel.*

62. *Double Portrait at a Clavichord* by Jan Barentsz Muyckens (1648). *The Hague, Gemeentemuseum.*

Herr E. Bach plays not only a very slow and songlike Adagio with the most touching expression . . . he is also able to sustain in this slow *tempo* a tone of six quavers duration with all degrees of power and softness; and this he can do in the bass as well as the treble. But he can accomplish it probably only on his precious Silbermann Clavichord, for which he has also specially written some Sonatas, in which he has introduced such long sustained tones. The same remark applies to the extraordinary power with which he renders some passages. Indeed it is the strongest *fortissimo*; and any other clavichords but Silbermann's would be knocked to pieces by it. And then again we have the most delicate *pianissimo* which it would be impossible to produce on any other clavichord.

A special type of clavichord, much used by organists, was that with pedals and two manuals. As organ practice necessitated being in church at times when it was unheated, and paying a servant to work the bellows, the pedal clavichord (and pedal harpsichord, and later the pedal pianoforte) provided the answer. Organ music could be played on it in the warmth of a private house, and needed the help

63.   Pedal clavichord by Johann Gerstenberg, 1760. *Leipzig, Musikinstrumenten-Museum in der Karl-Marx-Universität.*

of no other person. J.S. Bach's set of six *Trio-Sonatas* for organ could be played equally well on one of these instruments.

Pictures of the **harpsichord** appear from early in the fifteenth century, when it was known by variants of the Latin name *clavicymbalum*. It was virtually a keyed psaltery, and three different plucking mechanisms, as well as one for striking the strings, were described for it by Arnault. The action which became traditional, however, was as follows. When a key was pressed down its inner end would push up a wooden frame known as a 'jack', which contained a pivoted wooden tongue on which was a quill plectrum; when the jack rose the quill plucked the string, but avoided doing so on descent through the swinging back of the tongue. In 1698 Roger North emphasized the care needed in selecting quills for such instruments, when he wrote a letter 'concerning my cosen's espinette . . . if ever any new pens are put in, let'em not be stiff and hard, which spoyls all .

The earliest known shape of the harpsichord (as seen in plate 61), was used for the best instruments throughout its history, but there also existed, from the sixteenth century onwards, smaller and simpler shapes which were used primarily for domestic music. These instruments were covered indiscriminately by such names as 'virginal', 'spinet' and 'harpsichord', with little particularization of shape. Indeed, Praetorius summed up the situation under the title 'Spinetta (Italian, spinetto)':

In England all such instruments, whether large or small, are termed *Virginall*.
In France, *Espinettes*.
In the Netherlands, *Clavicymbel* and also *Virginall*.
In Germany, *Instrument*, like all other keyboard instruments.

Nowadays, however, the following general distinctions are used for convenience. **Virginal** or **virginals** applies to an instrument in which the strings usually run parallel to the keyboard. In northern Europe, particularly in England and the Low Countries during the period of Byrd, Bull and Sweelinck, the mechanism was built into a rectangular case from which it was not moved. In Italy, however, it had a light wooden frame, often polygonal in shape, which was frequently kept in a rectangular case but could be taken out of it at will. The **spinet**, built from the mid seventeenth century to *c*.1800, derived from this earlier Italian instrument (which had normally been called 'spineta') in that its shape was polygonal, and it often had at least one bent side. Its chief difference lay in its wrest plank being parallel to the keyboard, with the strings running at an oblique angle from left to right, as seen in plate 65. Both the spinet and the virginal generally had one string at 8′ pitch for each note, as did the early harpsichord and its upright version the **clavicytherium**. (Very small instruments were tuned at 4′ or 2′ pitch.) Double stringing on harpsichords, however, was already known to Arnault, and necessitated a second row of jacks, sometimes controlled by a stop lever to render it playable or silent. This second string was also at 8′ pitch, although by 1600 it had been replaced by a 4′ stop on certain instruments. Much use was made at this time of the bass 'short octave', a device which saved the instrument in size and cost. As the lowest chromatic notes were rarely needed, their keys were used to supplement the diatonic scale. A typical short octave, which can be seen in the harpsichord made by Jerome of Bologna in Rome in 1521 (now in the Victoria and Albert Museum, London) renders the apparent notes *E F♯ G♯* as *C D E*.

Such was the harpsichord during the first three-quarters of the sixteenth century, when, judging by surviving instruments, the chief makers were Italian. Then there became established in Antwerp the dynasty of Hans Ruckers (*c*.1550–*c*.1620) whose instruments, and those of his descendants, became the most prized in Europe. Their influence passed to France, where Nicolas Blanchet started a harpsichord-making business at Paris in 1686. This remained in the family when, in 1766, the widow of François Etienne Blanchet II married his apprentice Pascal Taskin. Few good harpsichords from Germany have survived until those of the eighteenth century, notably by the families of Hass, Silbermann and Stein. England imported many from abroad, although examples by John and Charles Haward point to good native work in the age of Purcell. From the 1720s onwards both Jacob Kirckmann of Germany and Burkat Shudi (Tschudi) of Switzerland

64. Virginals by Giovanni Celestini, Venice, 1593. *London, Royal College of Music.*

65. Spinet (view of soundboard) by John Crang, London, 1758. *London, Victoria and Albert Museum.*

67. Harpsichord by Jan Ruckers, Antwerp, 1638. Its two manuals are pitched a fourth apart, for transposing purposes. *Edinburgh, The Russell Collection of Harpsichords and Clavichords, St Cecilia's Hall.*

66. (Left) Clavicytherium, probably made in South Germany, *c*.1490. This is thought to be the oldest surviving stringed keyboard instrument. *London, Royal College of Music.*

worked in London, and together with Shudi's son-in-law John Broadwood they produced excellent harpsichords in their latest stages of development.

The growth of the harpsichord reflects in particular its place in the history of music. The single-manual instruments of the sixteenth century were quite adequate for the solo dances and abstract pieces of the time. As a continuo instrument, however, when the harpsichord was played more often with other instruments and with singers, a choice of pitch was sometimes needed. New instruments, the earliest ones dating from before 1600, were therefore built with two manuals, set at different pitches to ease transposition. From the mid seventeenth century, however, the construction was altered so that both manuals were tuned to the same pitch, and their respective stops could be sounded separately or coupled together for greater volume. An extra set of strings was often added to the existing two, resulting in an instrument where the upper manual controlled one 8′ stop, and the lower manual one at 8′ and one at 4′. This process of changing an existing instrument, including the extension of its compass to five octaves (often from F′), was largely carried out by the French makers, who called it

68.   Harpsichord by John Broadwood, London, 1793. This represents the
latest instruments before they gave way to the piano, having pedals for
machine stop and swell. The swell shutters are shown in their open position.
Edinburgh, The Russell Collection of Harpsichords and Clavichords,
St Cecilia's Hall.

ravalement. It made possible such compositions as Bach's *Italian Concerto*, which
could not be played effectively on a contemporary single-manual harpsichord.
    The instrument with two 8′ stops and one at 4′ was the basic requirement of the

eighteenth century. Other stops, however, were frequently added at this time to give greater variety to the sound, the rarest examples being registers at 2' and 16'. More usual were the *harp stop* (already known before 1700) which moved pads of buff leather up to the strings to create a *pizzicato* effect, and the *lute stop*, which, by having its jacks near to the nut of the instrument, produced a sound not unlike that of the lute. In England a *machine stop*, dating from about 1765, involved a pedal for the left foot which changed pre-arranged stops without the performer's hands leaving the keyboard. Pascal Taskin invented a similar device controlled by knee levers. He also used plectra of buff leather to give contrast to those of quill. Another difference to the usual *timbres* was produced by Johann Christoph Fleischer's **Lautenclavecin** of 1718, in which the strings of its two registers were of gut. Fleischer also made a **Theorbenflügel** with two registers of gut and one of metal.

With the appearance of the pianoforte, in which *crescendi* and *diminuendi* were no problem, efforts were made to render the harpsichord more expressive. The chief result was the *swell*. Already known on the organ, it appeared in the 1760s as the *Nag's Head Swell*, which involved part of the lid being raised by means of a pedal for the right foot. The *Venetian Swell*, patented by Shudi in 1769, also used such a pedal, which opened a row of shutters placed above the strings. It is significant that the machine stop and the swell were not present in the harpsichords of Bach, Handel and Domenico Scarlatti, and that these masters, while having at their disposal two manuals and several stops, could effect no *crescendi*, and had to change their registration by hand.

The harpsichord disappeared from music soon after 1800, but has been revived in the twentieth century. Some of these new instruments (particularly the most recent ones) are based as faithfully as possible on those of the past, while others have purposely been brought 'up to date'. Modern developments include regular 2' and 16' registers, a pedal to change each stop, and greater use of plectra of buff leather. Many instruments are made of more durable materials than before, to cope with travelling conditions and extreme changes of temperature resulting from concert tours.

Before considering the history of the pianoforte itself, we should note two instruments which foreshadowed it in their power of expression. One was the huge dulcimer made by Pantaleon Hebenstreit and known as the **Pantaleone** (see page 177). The other was the **Geigenwerk,** described in detail by Praetorius who said that it was invented by Hans Hayden of Nuremberg, who himself published a booklet about it in 1610. Of a similar shape to the harpsichord, it contained beneath its strings five or six rosined wheels which were set in motion by means of a pedal or bellows. According to Praetorius, 'when a key is depressed its accompanying string comes into contact with one of the revolving wheels, producing a sound as if a bow had been drawn over the string'. Varied dynamics could be produced from it, and, according to Hayden, it could be made to sound, among other things, like violins, a band of trumpets, a lute, hurdy-gurdy, shawm or bagpipes! Some examples had kettledrums attached, which were worked by their own stop.

69.   The Geigenwerk invented by Hans Hayden of Nuremberg. Praetorius, *Theatrum Instrumentorum* (Wolfenbuttel, 1620), Plate III.

In view of these and other developments, harpsichord makers in many parts of Europe were trying to make their instruments more expressive, and in the first two decades after 1700 various solutions were put forward involving the use of hammers instead of plectra. In 1708 the Frenchman Cuisinié made an instrument in which the strings were pressed down by hammers onto a revolving bow, and this may have influenced the hammer action in the *clavecin à maillets* produced by Jean Marius in 1716. In 1717 Christoph Gottlieb Schröter of Dresden, who knew Hebenstreit and the Pantaleone, devised a mechanism in which the strings could be struck from above or below. In fact all these attempts had been long foreshadowed by the fifteenth-century **dulce melos** in which, according to Arnault of Zwolle, the jacks were surmounted by pieces of lead instead of plectra, and the strings were therefore struck instead of plucked. Unfortunately the dulce melos did not survive.

It seems that the **pianoforte** (also called **fortepiano** in its early days, and henceforth in this book 'piano') itself originated in the Italian peninsula, and the man to whom the invention is generally accredited was Bartolomeo Cristofori (1655–1731), Keeper of Musical Instruments to Prince Ferdinand dei Medici at Florence. Cristofori's piano was seen in 1709 by the Marchese Scipione Maffei, who described it two years later in the *Giornale dei Letterati d'Italia*, but the invention is thought to date from before 1700. An inventory of the Prince's instruments in that year listed

> an *arpicembalo* of Bartolomeo Cristofori, a new invention, which plays *piano* and *forte* . . . with some dampers of red cloth touching the strings and some hammers which make the *piano* and *forte*.

The **gravicembalo col piano e forte**, as it was also known, was virtually a harpsichord but with hammers instead of plectra, and at first it was equipped with 'single action'. When a key was depressed, it pushed up an intermediate lever on which was pivoted a hopper (escapement). This in turn hit the hammer which hit the string, and at the same time a damper was moved from the string, leaving it free to vibrate. (The hammer butt then rested on the edge of the pivoted hopper a short distance away, and its shank was supported by crossed silken threads.) When the

70. Piano by Bartolomeo Cristofori, Florence, 1720. *New York, Metropolitan Museum of Art, Crosby Brown Collection.*

key was released, the damper, hammer and hopper returned to their original positions. After further experimentation Cristofori produced a 'double action', which survives in his piano of 1726, now in the Musical Instrument Museum of the Karl Marx University, Leipzig. On this the hopper was hinged to the key itself, with the intermediate lever between it and the hammer. When the hammer had struck the string, it fell back to a check which held it in position until the key was released. This mechanism had several advanges over the single action. Firstly, the hammer had a greater chance of hitting the right pair of strings than before, due to having a shorter upward journey. Secondly, for the same reason, there was greater control over the quality of tone produced, particularly in soft passages. Thirdly, the hammer would not bounce back and accidentally hit the string again. Cristofori also made an *una corda* device, which, controlled by hand, shifted the mechanism so that only one string at a time was played upon, thereby producing a softer sound. In 1732 there appeared in Florence the first music published especially for the piano, a set of sonatas composed by D. Lodovico Giustini of Pistoia, and dedicated to Prince Antonio of Portugal, a pupil of Domenico Scarlatti.

The first important maker of pianos in Germany was Gottfried Silbermann of Saxony. Like Cristofori he used double action, and in 1736 showed one of his pianos to J.S. Bach for an opinion. Bach observed that the treble was too weak, but 11 years later gave his approval to a more balanced design, although himself still preferring to play on the older keyboard instruments. Royal patronage came from Frederick II of Prussia (later the Emperor Frederick the Great), who bought several Silbermann pianos to install in his palaces.

The next landmark in the development of the mechanism was the 'German' or 'Viennese action' attributed to Johann Andreas Stein of Augsburg, c.1770. Here the hammer was connected to the key itself, while the escapement was on a separate frame. The resulting tone was more even than that of the Silbermann pianos, and needed a lighter touch. It was exactly right for the music of Mozart, who praised Stein's instruments in a letter written to his father on 17–18 October 1777, adding

> He himself [Stein] told me that when he has finished making one of these claviers, he sits down to it and tries all kinds of passages, runs and jumps, and he polishes and works away at it until it can do anything. For he labours solely in the interests of music and not for his own profit; otherwise he would soon finish the work.

Meanwhile a small rectangular instrument, known as the 'square' piano, was designed c.1740 for those people who would previously have had a spinet rather than a harpsichord. (The earliest one known to exist was made by Johann Söcher of Swabia in 1742, and is now in the Germanisches Nationalmuseum at Nuremberg.) Its greatest period of popularity seems to have been after Johannes Zumpe, a former pupil of Silbermann, settled in London in 1760 to work with Shudi. His instruments were small and economical, and, unlike his former master, Zumpe preferred to use single action. According to Burney, writing in Rees's *Cyclopaedia*

71. Square piano by Clementi & Co., London, c.1825. *London, Royal College of Music.*

'he could not make them fast enough to gratify the craving of the public'. The first public piano recital in England was given by Johann Christian Bach on a Zumpe square piano in 1768. The adaptability of such instruments can be seen from an anecdote, recounted in the reminiscences of the singer Michael Kelly, about Richard Brinsley Sheridan coming to dinner to discuss plans for songs and choruses in drama:

> After the cloth was removed, he proposed business. I had pen, ink, music-paper and a small piano-forte (which the Duke of Queensberry had given me and which he had been accustomed to take with him in his carriage when he travelled) put upon the table with our wine.

Double action for the English square piano was patented by the German-born John Geib in 1786.

While Silbermann's pupil Zumpe was largely responsible for the success of the square piano in England, another of his disciples who had gone to London, the Dutchman Americus Backers, had a considerable influence on the development of the grand piano. Together with the Englishman Robert Stodart and the Scot John Broadwood, he invented in or after 1772 the 'English grand action' which was based to a great extent on that of Cristofori, and had better control than before on the descent of the hammers. The earliest use of this action seems to have been in a combined harpsichord and piano made by Stodart in 1777. Broadwood, who had arrived in London in 1761 to work with Shudi, and later married his daughter Barbara, used it in his own grand pianos, of which the first is dated 1781. By this time the *una corda* and sustaining effects were no longer worked by hand, and therefore did not impede performance. In pianos by Stein, Taskin and others, these devices took the form of knee levers, while instruments by Backers and

72.   Grand piano by Pascal-Joseph I. Taskin, Paris, 1788; its sustaining and
una corda effects are obtained by means of knee levers below the keyboard.
Paris, Conservatoire National Supérieur de Musique.

Broadwood had foot pedals (still used today) adapted from those of the machine
stop and swell of the late harpsichord. The left pedal made the music softer by
moving a soft pad up to the strings, while the right one raised the dampers to
sustain the sounds.‘

As the earliest pianos were made to the proportions of the harpsichord, they
were inadequate for the tension produced by the hammer mechanism. The
wooden frame had therefore to be strengthened, and by the late eighteenth century
onwards it was increasingly supported by metal. Broadwood's grand pianos were
among the first to be made larger and heavier than before, being extended to six
octaves. They were well suited to the dramatic music of Beethoven, whose

73. Upright piano by Priestly, London, c.1860; its case is painted by Edward Burne-Jones. *London, Victoria and Albert Museum.*

powerful playing often broke the strings of delicate instruments, and in 1818 the composer gladly accepted a piano from the firm which by then was known as John Broadwood and Sons. The first completely iron frame was made for a square piano by Alpheus Babcock of Boston, Massachusetts, in 1825. Not until 1851 did the complete iron frame appear in a Broadwood grand (built for the Great Exhibition at Crystal Palace), and four years later in one by Steinway and Sons of New York. (Heinrich Steinweg had moved from Germany to America in 1848 and had altered his name.) By 1859 Steinway had adapted to the grand piano the technique of overstringing (apparently invented in 1833 by Bridgeland and Jardine of New York), in which the strings are not all in the same plane as before, but are arranged in two parallel rows. This not only saved the space required by the strings, but also balanced the tension.

74. Grand piano by Steinway and Sons, New York and Hamburg, 1963,
played by Frank Merrick. *London, Royal College of Music.*

Two important developments occurred towards the end of Beethoven's lifetime. The first was the 'double escapement' action invented by Sébastien Erard in
1821. By this means the hammer did not need to fall back to its base before the
note could be played again; as long as the key was depressed the hammer remained
poised near the string, and was enabled by the mechanism to strike it again more
rapidly than had hitherto been possible. The other event was the introduction, by
Henri Pape of Paris in 1826, of felt hammers to replace the leather ones used before.

Already in the eighteenth century certain grand pianos had been made in an
upright position, with their strings rising upwards from the level of the keyboard,
as in the old clavicytherium. In 1798 this idea was applied to the square piano by
William Southwell of Dublin, who set its own soundboard in a vertical position.
In 1800 the Englishman John Isaac Hawkins, working in Philadelphia, and the
German Matthias Müller of Vienna separatedly invented pianos in which the
strings were perpendicular to the ground, and nearly reached it. Following these
came William Southwell's **Cabinet Piano** (1807), and in 1811 Robert Wornum of

London produced his **Cottage Piano.** This set the basic pattern for the traditional uprights which finally superseded the square pianos. These later grew larger, but a popular small model appeared in the 1930s in the form of Percy Brasted's **Minipiano**, based on a miniature instrument by Lundholm of Stockholm. From time to time the piano has been furnished with stops to give different effects, the 'Turkish percussion' instruments being a favourite adjunct. The player piano, in which music is produced by means of paper rolls, is described in chapter IX among the mechanical instruments.

Pianos of today have been considerably strengthened since those of the mid nineteenth century, one of the most recent developments being Alfred Knight's incorporation of worthy plastic materials into the mechanism. The strings, which were originally in pairs and later sometimes triple, are now single and very thick in the bass, double in the middle and triple for the thin strings of the upper register. Most pianos have a compass of seven octaves from A'' to a'''', while some extend to c''''''. A third pedal, invented by C. Montal in 1862 to sustain low chords below freely-moving upper parts, is used today in Steinway pianos, but has not been universally adopted. The third quarter of the twentieth century has produced methods of playing inside the piano (see page 187), thus opening up a completely new range of sounds undreamt of by Bartolomeo Cristofori.

— CHAPTER IV —
Organs

During the Hellenistic period one of the chief centres of scientific discovery was Alexandria, and it is believed to have been there that the organ was invented, in the middle of the 3rd century BC, by the engineer Ktesibios.

Using the syrinx as his model for arranging the pipes, Ktesibios devized the **hydraulis**, which was described in detail by Hero of Alexandria in the 1st century AD. Air was pumped by one man into a perforated vessel (*pnigeus*) standing in a cistern of water, and from the *pnigeus* it was further directed into the windchest below the pipes, pressure from the water maintaining its steadiness. The pitch was determined by any key, which, when pressed, set in motion a slider between the pipes and the windchest. When a hole in the slider came into contact with the lower end of the pipe, the air from below was released to cause a sound. Vitruvius, writing at about the same time as Hero, described a more advanced hydraulis which had two pumps working alternately and at least four ranks of flue or reed pipes. The number of ranks determined the number of holes in the sliders.

From the beginning, when it was played by Thaïs, the wife of Ktesibios, the hydraulis attracted considerable attention, and in 90 BC was one of the instruments used in a musical festival at Delphi, in honour of Apollo. Evidence of it in Rome dates from the 1st century AD, when one of its outstanding performers was the emperor Nero, who may himself have been responsible for its importation from Greece.

The hydraulis was a large instrument, but by the 2nd century AD there had emerged a smaller organ into which air was pumped by bellows. It had no water to compress the air, so its pressure was at first unsteady, until an air reservoir (possibly of leather) was added. Such a **pneumatic organ** dated 228 was excavated in 1931 at the Roman settlement of Aquincum near Budapest, but its perishable parts had been destroyed in a fire. Enough remained, however, to permit a partial reconstruction, showing that the instrument had four ranks of 13 flue pipes. Three of the ranks were 'stopped' at the top, producing lower notes than if they were open. According to a remark by Bishop Theodoret of Cyrrhus (387–450) (quoted by Perrot, p. 63) it seems that the performer of a pneumatic organ would sometimes work the bellows with his feet.

After the Barbarian invasions and the recession of the greater Roman Empire in the 5th century the organ was forgotten in most of Europe, but it remained in the

75. Hydraulis, made as a clay lamp. Roman, 2nd or 3rd century AD. *London, British Museum.*

76.　Organ, with three men treading on the bellows. Above it are a horn, an early type of gittern, and crotales. Illustration of Psalm 150 from the *Stuttgart Psalter*, made in France, *c.*830. *Stuttgart, Wurttembergische Landesbibliothek, MS. Bibl. fol.23, f.163v.*

Eastern Empire centred on Constantinople (Byzantium), where it was particularly associated with imperial entrances and exits, but was not by custom played in church.

When, as part of a diplomatic gesture, the Byzantine Emperor Constantine Copronymus sent an organ to King Pepin the Short of the Franks in 757, it was hailed by the chroniclers as being hitherto unknown in France. After 826, when the Venetian priest Georgius built an organ for Louis the Pious at Aix-la-Chapelle, the instrument gradually spread through Europe. Only from the tenth century, however, is there much evidence of its use in church, at first just for important feast-days and special celebrations. Among many known organs of this period was one given by St Dunstan (*c.*924–88) to the abbey at Malmesbury. The abbey of Fleury (St Benoît-sur-Loire) acquired one *c.*1077, and Canterbury Cathedral is known to have had one in the north aisle of the nave at the time of a fire in 1114. That at St Peter's, Winchester, is the best known from this early period, due to a detailed but somewhat imaginative poem written about it by the monk Wulstan to Bishop Elphege II of Winchester in or after 984.

From the eleventh century there survive two important treatises giving detailed instructions for the building of church organs. One is by Theophilus, a monk who lived in Germany or eastern France, and the author of the other is known as the Anonymous of Berne, although he is thought to have been a monk at Fleury. Both writers specify pipes of copper, but those of Theophilus are conical in shape and those of the Anonymous cylindrical. While Theophilus has slow-moving sliders which need to be pulled out to produce a note, the Anonymous has keys with a spring mechanism (similar to that of Hero) enabling them to return automatically to their original position. These and other sources indicate that the names of the notes were often written on or by the sliders or keys, and that B♭ was the only accidental, the range being approximately one to three octaves. The number of bellows and blowers varied according to the size of each organ.

Although Theophilus suggested placing the organ high up in an arcade, organ lofts were not frequently built until the fourteenth century, by which time some of the instruments were very large, this type eventually becoming known as the

77. Two portative organs (showing front and back views) played with tambourine and fiddle in the anonymous Florentine *Musical Angels* of *c*.1350. *Oxford, Christ Church Picture Gallery.*

78. Portative organ with chromatic keys. Detail from *The Mystic Marriage of St Catherine* by Hans Memling (*c.*1435–94). *Bruges, Hôpital St Jean.*

great organ. The smaller **positive organ**, which also needed separate people to work the bellows and play on the keyboard, could be moved about between performances and was sometimes adjacent to the great organ in order to provide contrasting sounds. The positive, however, was not restricted to church use, and was frequently used for secular occasions, as was the even smaller **portative organ**. This was played entirely by one person, who worked the bellows with one hand and played on the keyboard with the other. The keys were either button-shaped or flat, and the technique of playing varied somewhat according to each type. The portative organ (**organetto** in Italy) normally had from one to three ranks of pipes, and many pictures show large drones which could be sounded throughout the music if needed. The origin of this small organ is uncertain, but it only became widespread in the visual arts *c*.1300.

Until this time all organ pipes had to be above their own sliders or keys, so that the air could rise directly upwards. Wide pipes needed wide keys, which were heavy and sometimes had to be pressed down by a whole fist. The fourteenth-century invention of rollers rendered this unnecessary, as they enabled the 'tracker' action of rods and wires to be directed sideways and the pipes placed further away from the keyboard. Hence the number of pipes could be greatly increased and the keys themselves reduced in width, each becoming easily playable by one finger, allowing for much faster playing. Small positives with narrow pipes and keys did not always need such devices (nor did many portatives), and it may have been for such an instrument that there was written the earliest known keyboard music, the dances and song arrangements in the so-called Robertsbridge Fragment (British Library MS Add. 28550) dating from *c*.1325. These call for at least four chromatic notes, coinciding with the increase of 'black keys' in fourteenth-century pictures until completely chromatic keyboards were available *c*.1400.

Although most mediaeval organs had several ranks of pipes to each note, they could not be detached from each other. Hence the sound was a great 'mixture' of diapason unisons, fifths and octaves, which in Germany became known as the *Blockwerk*. Then other departments were added in the Netherlands and Germany, the first being the pedals and the positive. Lodewijk van Valbecke of Louvain (d. *c*.1312) is said to have been the first to use pedal keys for low notes, but at first they just pulled down the lower keys of the manual. Soon afterwards they became an independent part having their own pipes. The positive organ which had sometimes been placed by the great was now installed behind the organist's back. He could either turn round to perform on it, or, if the action passed beneath his feet, he could play on it from a second keyboard under that of the main instrument. This department became known as the *Rückpositiv*, one of its earliest examples being at Utrecht Cathedral *c*.1400. Basically a great organ could sound at 8′ pitch, the positive at 4′ and the pedals at 16′, although this was not a fixed rule. Sometimes two manuals could be 'coupled' together to sound simultaneously (this was already known at Rouen Cathedral in 1386), even though only one was being played upon.

It seems to have been around 1400 that drawstops were re-invented to separate the different ranks within each department, but it was a long time before they

79. Organ designed for tracker action. Thought to have come from the Abondance Abbey in Savoy, this is the oldest European organ known to be in playing condition; parts of it date from *c*.1380. *Sion, Cathedral of Notre Dame de Valère.*

80. (Above) Positive organ with a
few chromatic notes. Detail from a
Psalter made in England for the
Bohun family, c.1370–80. *London,
British Library, MS. Eg. 3277, f.67.*

81. (Above right) Positive organ
with pedals. Detail from *The Seven
Planets Series – Mercury* by Hans
Sebald Beham (1500–1550).

82. (Right) Organ by Lorenzo di
Giacomo da Prato, made between
1474–83, and with subsequent
alterations. It is the oldest
surviving organ known to have had
separate ranks of pipe from the
beginning. *Bologna, Church of San
Petronio.*

were widely used, Arnault of Zwolle (*c.*1440) describing organs only of the *Blockwerk* type. In Germany and Flanders these stops served to detach certain registers from the *Blockwerk*, while in Italy they enabled each rank to be played separately. The earliest surviving organ of the latter type was built between 1474 and 1483 by Lorenzo di Giacomo da Prato for the church of San Petronio, Bologna. Some instruments, however, kept the *Blockwerk* system for the great organ and used a positive for the independent stops, the Haarlem church of St Bavo retaining its organ like this until 1630.

During the fifteenth century there appeared also the **regal**, a small organ with reeds, which may have been invented by Heinrich Traxdorff of Nuremberg, *c.*1460. Its pitch was determined not so much by the length of the resonators, which were very small, but by the thickness and length of the beating reeds. The name *regal* was also given to the reed stop itself, and to some organs containing both flues and reeds. One of the 'regalles' of Henry VIII had 'one Stoppe of pipes of woode a Cimbell of Tinne and a Regall'. (The cymbel is a high-sounding mixture stop.)

Renaissance and Baroque organs developed distinct national styles, of which the most progressive were those of northern Germany and the Netherlands. Their interweaving polyphonic music demanded that each melodic line should, if needed, be distinguished from the others, and so many new stops were invented,

83. Regal, probably German; early 17th century. *London, Royal College of Music.*

based to a great extent on the sounds of other instruments; the first to appear was that of the flute. A typical German organ of the Renaissance was described by the Heidelberg organist and composer Arnolt Schlick in his *Spiegel der Orgelmacher und Organisten* (Speyer, 1511). Instruments imitated in its stops include the gemshorn, flageolet, Rauschpfeife, Zinck (cornett), crumhorn, trumpet or trombone, and a percussion sound which 'resembles that of a small boy hitting a pot with a spoon'. (The trumpet or trombone stop was played by the pedals.)

Soon further departments were added, each one containing the basic requirements of the diapason chorus (the remains of the *Blockwerk*), flutes and reeds, and having its own manual. In addition to the *Hauptwerk* (great), *Rückpositiv* and pedals, a section known as the *Brustwerk* (by its position just above the breast of the organist) was added below the great, and also one above the great, the *Oberwerk*. In certain elaborate Rococo designs, such as that by J. Gabler at

84. Organ showing a *Rückpositiv* behind the organist's seat. Praetorius, *Theatrum Instrumentorum*, (1620) Plate II.

Weingarten (1737–50), there is even a *Kronwerk* above that. It was not necessary, however, for each organ to have all these departments. The music of Bach, for instance, needed only two manuals and pedalboard, such as can be found in the organ now at Capel in Jutland, rebuilt in 1695 by the celebrated Arp Schnitger, whose instruments represent the summit of excellence and versatility in North Germany. Gottfried Silbermann attained a similar if somewhat more stereotyped result in the south.

In contrast to the Germanic and Netherlandish organs, those of Italy remained simple, the Renaissance instruments being best represented by those of the Antegnati family at Brescia. An average instrument would have only one manual, with a soft principal chorus, and sometimes the slightly off-pitch *fiffaro* with which this undulated. Pedals, when they existed, were pull-downs. Two-manual organs were rare, one being that by D. Benvenuti and F. Palmieri (1585–7) in the church of Santa Maria in Aracoeli, Rome. Here there was a *Rückpositiv* containing a *Regale* stop (both rare in Italy) besides, on the first manual, stops for the effects of drums and birds which were becoming popular in many parts of Europe. Apart from the flute, few other instruments had been named in Italian stops before this time. Their increase during the seventeenth century was largely due to foreign craftsmen such as the Silesian organ-builder Johann Caspar, who changed his name to Eugenio Casparini. His organ built in 1694 for a church at Merano contained such Italianate names as *Superottava* and *Vigesimaseconda* together with the German *Nachthorn* and *Gemsflöte*.

Organs of Renaissance France varied in style, some being of the simple Italian type, and others reflecting the long-standing artistic influence of Flanders. There soon developed, however, a definite French organ which was described in detail by Dom Bédos de Celles in his *L'Art du Facteur d'Orgues* (Paris, 1766–78). It often had two manuals and pedals, and the stops, among which reeds were prominent, became so standardized that such composers as de Grigny, Clérambault and François Couperin were able to specify exactly which were to be used. (In other countries this was unusual due to the individuality of each organ, and variety of registration was expected.)

Spain was also influenced to a certain extent by its Flemish connections, producing organs with two manuals and pedals, and stops imitating other instruments, besides special effects such as 'an unusual device of bells, suitable for the Elevation of the Host' which appeared in an organ by Mathieu Telles for the cathedral of Lérida in 1554. One of the chief characteristics of Spanish organs was the strength of their reeds, emphasized in the Baroque period by dramatic trumpet pipes projecting horizontally in front of the organ. It was in Spain that the swellbox originated. Previously the different ranks had by their very nature been contrasted, and the placing of certain pipes in a closed box had produced an echo effect. In late seventeenth-century Spain a foot lever enabled the lid of such a box to be opened and shut, thereby making the sound progressively louder and softer.

English organs were for a long time similar to those of Italy, having one manual, no pedal pipes (although pull-downs may occasionally have been used) and stops which were mainly diapasons with the addition of a flute or recorder. Thomas

85. Organ by Gottfried Silbermann, 1710–14. *Freiberg Cathedral, D.D.R.*

Dallam's organ at King's College, Cambridge (1606) may have been the first English one to have two manuals, as did his organ in Worcester Cathedral (1613), which had a 'chaire' ('choir') organ, equivalent to the *Rückpositiv*. A new age of organ-building began with the Restoration in 1660, after the Commonwealth in which so many organs had been destroyed, or removed to other places. (That from Rochester Cathedral had been transferred to a tavern in Greenwich, to cite one example of such a move.) New ideas from the Continent were incorporated into the designs of 'Father' Bernard Smith and his younger rival Renatus Harris. Smith introduced the echo organ to England (at the Temple Church in 1683), while Harris built the first four-manual English organ at Salisbury Cathedral in 1710. Both introduced Continental stops which were new to England. Although Harris included six manuals, a pedalboard and a swell mechanism in a grandiose scheme for St Paul's Cathedral, this instrument was never built. It was left to Abraham Jordan to introduce a swellbox (different from the Iberian type) at the church of St Magnus the Martyr, London Bridge, in 1712. Among the first authenticated pedals (even these were pull-downs) in an English church were those in the organ at St Mary Redcliffe, Bristol, built by John Harris, a son of Renatus, and his brother-in-law John Byfield I in 1726. Later in the century the best English organs were built by the Swiss settler Johann Snetzler and by George England, who, with his son George Pike England, worked in the traditions of Renatus Harris.

English organs, however, were still conservative, and when Mendelssohn visited London in 1829 he could not find one on which to play the music of Bach. It was William Hill, together with Dr Henry John Gauntlett, who, by insisting on independent pedal pipes, at last made this possible. Hill also improved the swell mechanism and added new stops, such as the *Grand Ophicleide* at Birmingham Town Hall in 1837, before completing his masterpiece for the George Street Chapel, Liverpool, in 1841. While remaining in the classical tradition, Hill can be said to have brought the English organ up to date.

In the same year, however, Aristide Cavaillé-Coll, the creator of the French Romantic Organ, came to prominence when he built an instrument for the abbey of St Denis. His aim was to produce an instrument of great expressiveness and symphonic proportions, in keeping with the taste of the day. In doing so he certainly produced an organ capable of playing French Romantic music, but *in*capable of playing authentically anything composed for the instrument before that time. He excluded, for instance, the mutation stops which had been a feature of classical organs (only bringing them back in later years at the request of such scholarly organists as Saint-Saens and Guilmant), and made a feature of dramatic reed choruses, arranging his trumpets horizontally (*en chamade*) as in Spain. With a ventil system he caused great *crescendi* and *diminuendi* by bringing into action progressively more ranks while still playing, and since this involved much coupling together of manuals, he used the pneumatic action developed by Charles Spackman Barker in 1832. This caused a lighter touch on the manuals than if the whole instrument were worked by tracker action. One of Cavaillé-Coll's best known organs was that at the church of Sainte Clothilde in Paris, where for many years the organist was César Franck.

86.   Organ by Aristide Cavaillé-Coll, 1859; it was played upon for many years by César Franck. *Paris, Church of Ste Clothilde.*

87.   Organ designed by Ralph Downes and built by Harrison & Harrison of Durham, 1954. *London, Royal Festival Hall.*

The Romantic Organ came to prominence in England at the Great Exhibition of 1851, with the work of Henry Willis and the German Edmund Schulze. Willis was then commissioned to build an organ for St George's Hall, Liverpool, an instrument which, when completed, was one of the most progressive of its day, containing numerous devices for simplifying the action. These included thumb pistons, which when pressed during performance could change several pre-arranged stops at once; also pneumatic lever action, and a steam engine to help with the wind supply. The pedal board was concave and radiating, an arrangement which came into widespread but not universal use. This organ was played upon for many years by W.T. Best, who was renowned for performing arrangements of orchestral works at a time when concerts were comparatively rare. Willis's organ at Canterbury Cathedral (1886) was one of the first to be activated on a large scale by electricity. The family firm of Willis survives to this day, as do other nineteenth-century dynasties such as those of Walker, and Harrison and Harrison.

The chief developments of the present century have stemmed from the Classical

88.   Claviorganum by Lodewijk Theeuwes, London, 1579. *London, Victoria and Albert Museum.*

Revival in Germany in the 1920s (the *Orgelbewegung*), resulting in the building of organs in the Baroque style (some with tracker action), and the restoration of countless early ones to their original condition. These organs, however, were not made for Romantic music, so the next step was to build large ones containing the ingredients necessary for music of all periods. In England the process was in reverse. No significant return to classical principles had taken place until, in a clean break with ultraconservatism, there appeared in 1954 the organ of the Royal Festival Hall, London. Designed by Ralph Downes and voiced under his direction, it was built by the Durham firm of Harrison and Harrison. Here there are to be found the chief principles of the German *Orgelbewegung* together with the best features of English, Dutch and French organ design of the nineteenth century. Although its actions are electro-pneumatic, it has proved to be more than adequate for the stylish performance of any kind of organ music.

The economic depression of the early 1970s, coinciding with a desire for organs reproducing as faithfully as possible those of the Renaissance and Baroque periods, has resulted in a record vintage of small encased organs with light tracker

89. Lira organizzata or organ hurdy-gurdy, possibly made by a Frenchman living in London; 18th century. *London, Victoria and Albert Museum.*

actions. In spite of their size they have a strong carrying power which in large buildings reintroduces a perspective and dimension long since forgotten. The clear response of their tone and mechanism has led to a marked improvement in the standard of organ playing today. Inevitably, however, they are unsuitable for the performance of Romantic works, as they were not intended for such music. The solution can be found in a building which already possesses a good organ of the late nineteenth or early twentieth century. By the preservation of this and the acquisition of a new organ with tracker action, the organ repertoire can be performed as faithfully as possible.

Before leaving the organ, mention should be made of some of the ways in which it has been combined with other instruments. In the Renaissance and Baroque **claviorganum** it was coupled to a harpsichord, and as such was heard by Burney

90. Piano-organ with bottles instead of pipes, by Johann Samuel Kühlewein of Eisleben, 1798. *Liverpool, City Museum.*

as the accompaniment to nuns' voices in Rome. As the **lira organizzata** it became one with the hurdy-gurdy, and was fashionable at the court of Naples in Haydn's day. As the **barrel organ** it was combined with the mechanical cylinder and used in churches from about 1700 onwards. Perhaps the most curious example is the **piano-organ** made by Johann Samuel Kühlewein of Eisleben in 1798 for a church in Heligoland. Combining organ pipes and the mechanism of a piano, its chief interest is in the 'pipes'. The inaccessibility of the island during winter months would have prevented an organ builder from coming over from the mainland to do repairs, so Kühlewein substituted for the more orthodox pipes an ingenious arrangement of glass bottles, ranging in diameter from 6″ to ¼″, and all carefully tuned by the insertion of an appropriate amount of wax. This curious hybrid is to be seen today in the City Museum, Liverpool.

— CHAPTER V —
The Woodwind Families

In *The House of Fame* Chaucer said that 'soun ys nocht but eyr ybroken'. Air can be broken in countless different ways, and it is according to these that instruments are classified. Among woodwind instruments (made not only of wood but also of bone, metal, and more recently of plastic) these methods can be summarized as the pressure of air against (a) a sharp edge in the instrument itself, or (b) a reed or two reeds at the upper end. While the word 'pipe' covers them all generically, 'flute' applies only to those in the first category. Wind instruments in general are classified as *aerophones*.

In early days Man discovered that he could produce a sound by blowing across one end of a tube, and then he found that pipes of different lengths became deeper in pitch as they became longer. By fixing a set of such pipes together, the ancients devised the **syrinx**, also known through its association with the god Pan as **pan-pipes**.

91. Phrygian pipes, and panpipes, played in a Bacchanalian scene on a Gallo-Roman relief found at Vaison. *Avignon, Musée Calvet.*

It was also found that a single pipe with fingerholes could produce different notes according to the placing of the fingers, and this principle became used in various ways. One is seen in the transverse flute, where the sound is produced by air blown directly against the edge of the mouth-hole. Another involves the insertion of a wooden block (fipple) into the top of an end-blown pipe, leaving only a narrow air passage. Below the fipple is cut a small window, its lower edge set to break the oncoming air. Pipes in this category are known as *duct flutes*, and include flageolets, tabor pipes, recorders, gemshorns and pitch pipes, besides bird whistles and ocarinas where the duct is fashioned out of such material as clay.

92. Bird whistle from a settlement at Spina, near Ferrara, *c.*500 BC. The player blows through a hole in the bird's tail, and by covering the hole in each wing, can produce the sound of a cuckoo. This instrument is the direct ancestor of the cuckoo used in toy symphonies. *London, Author's Collection.*

Of these the most simple is the **pitch pipe**, which was designed to give a single note to church choirs and was used mainly in the eighteenth and nineteenth centuries. The bottom end of the pipe held a stopper which, when moved up or down by one hand, altered the sounding length of the pipe to give the required note.

In the one-man combination of the **pipe-and-tabor** the left hand plays on a pipe while the right hand accompanies on a drum suspended from the left arm. The pipe has two finger holes in front and a thumb hole at the back, and about two octaves can be obtained from it by over-blowing. Dating from around 1200 in pictorial sources, it was played until the Renaissance in all strata of society, but is now used mainly in folk music. In England it is played by Morris dancers on such occasions as the May Morning revels in Oxford, after the choir of Magdalen College has sung on top of the Chapel tower at 6 a.m.

The **gemshorn** was a late mediaeval and early Renaissance horn with fingerholes, being blown from its wide end which was blocked up to leave only a narrow air passage. It was particularly associated with Germanic countries.

From the Middle Ages onwards the word **flageolet** has been used for a whistle pipe with an unstandardized number of holes, such as can be traced back to Antiquity. The instrument is mentioned in mediaeval poems as providing the music for dancing, and Pepys, who carried a 'flagelette' around with him, played it in such situations as when, on 9 February 1660,

. . . Swan and I to a drinking-house near Temple-bar; where while he writ, I played of my flagelette till a dish of poached eggs was got ready for us.

93. Pipe-and-tabor, played by a man dressed as a devil; from a margin of the *Smithfield Decretals*, written in Italy but illustrated in England, *c*.1325–50. *London, British Library MS Roy. 10.E.iv, f.201v.*

94. (Above right) Gemshorn, held by one of the skeletons in the *Dance of Death*, illustrated by Heinrich Knoblochtzer, Strassburg, *c*.1488. *Heidelberg, University Library.*

95. Two flageolets from the frontispiece of Thomas Greeting's *Pleasant Companion*, London, 1682. The source from which this plate was taken is a profusely extra-illustrated copy of: *Samuel Pepys, Diary and correspondence of . . . with a life and notes by Richard Ld. Bolingbroke . . . Notes by Mynors Bright.* (London, 1879), Vol. VI, between pages 2 and 3. *Los Angeles, William Andrews Clark Memorial Library.*

This may have been a pipe with two thumbholes and four fingerholes which was chiefly associated with France, or a similar one used also in England for teaching birds to sing. Tunes for such a **bird pipe** were published by Richard Meares in the *Bird Fancyer's Delight* (1717), where excerpts from *The Beggar's Opera* and other popular sources were set for 'Ye Wood-lark, Black-bird, Throustill, House-sparrow, Canary-bird' and others. Nineteenth-century flageolets included such varied instruments as the single, double or triple pipes invented by William Bainbridge, and the tiny **Picco pipe** first made by the Italian shepherd Picco; at the present time the word brings to mind the 'penny whistle', although as inflation goes it will never again cost a penny.

The early history of the **recorder** is uncertain for several reasons. One is that the word itself seems to date from a later period than the earliest surviving examples, so the instrument may previously have been covered by the ambiguous 'whistle' (Latin *fistula*) or 'pipe'. We cannot be sure what was meant when, as late as 1419, the will of Stephen Thomas of Leigh, Essex, left to Thomas Chesse 'my best gown of the King's livery that is at home at my house, and my gold ring, and my whistle'. Another difficulty is in identifying the recorder from the visual arts. Many pictures only show the front view of an instrument, so it is impossible to see if the necessary thumbhole is intended to be present. Even if it is, its existence still cannot be proved if the thumb is actually covering it. One picture which does *not* show a recorder is that from the twelfth-century Psalter from York (Glasgow University Library, MS U.3.2, f.21v.), which has led several authorities to give it that name on account of its shape. However, M.H. Armstrong Davison, in 'A Note on the History of the Northumbrian Small Pipes' (*GSJ* XXII, 1969, 78–80) has shown without doubt that there is a small bag leading from the top end of the pipe, and tucked under the performer's arm. This is clearly seen by looking at the manuscript itself, or at a colour reproduction.

The earliest known reference to the word *recorder* appears in an account book of the house of Henry, Earl of Derby (later Henry IV), where payment is made for a 'fistula nomine Ricordo' (as observed by Brian Trowell in 'King Henry IV, Recorder-player', *GSJ* X, 1957, 83–4). We can only hope that this satisfied the necessary requirements for the instrument, namely that it should be a duct flute with a thumbhole at the back and seven fingerholes in front. In early examples two holes were set for the little finger, depending on whether the player was right- or left-handed, and the unused hole was blocked up with wax. These ingredients are all present in a mediaeval recorder excavated at the *Huis te Merwede* near Dordrecht, and now kept in the Gemeentemuseum at The Hague. One curious feature for such an early instrument is that each end is shaped to form a tenon, but the pieces which should have been attached to them have not survived. Experiments have shown that with an added foot joint the bottom note would have been about c''.

During the fifteenth century the recorder was increasingly made in different sizes with a view to consort playing, and pictures from that time often show three being played together. After the bass of the family appeared *c*.1500 (it was shown by Virdung in 1511), a consort could consist of descant, treble (alto), tenor and

bass, although the descant was often omitted in favour of another of the more mellow instruments. The pitch varied from one set to another, but being relative to $fc'f'c''$ from the bass upwards. (The recorder, however, is a transposing instrument and its music is written an octave lower.) The 1547 inventory of Henry VIII's instruments refers to a 'greate base Recorder of woode', but its pitch is not known. By the time of Praetorius the sizes ranged from a great bass in F to a sopranino ('Exilent') in g'', with an alternative pitch for each size. Praetorius himself suggested making recorders in two sections to remedy tuning problems, but this idea was not widely adopted at the time. It finally became widespread after 1650, probably through the work of Jean Hotteterre the Elder, a wind player to Louis XIV and expert maker and repairer of instruments. The new recorders were in three sections: the head joint containing the mouthpiece and window, the tapering middle joint with six fingerholes, and the foot joint with one hole for the little finger, sometimes controlled by a key. This joint could be turned round to suit the player, so the old extra hole became redundant. While the Renaissance recorder with its wide cylindrical bore had a mellow tone which blended well for the consort music of its period, the new Baroque instrument gave a more penetrating sound, capable of holding its own in Bach's *Second Brandenburg Concerto*. The treble was used for this, and for most solo work and trio sonatas. The recorder family as a whole, however, was unsuitable for the expressive music being written from c.1750 onwards, as it could not grow much louder or softer without becoming out of tune. It gave way, therefore, to the transverse flute, and had to

96. (Left) Recorders (?) of three sizes and below them, from left to right, a harp, dulcimer and lute; detail from the Flemish painting *Mary Queen of Heaven* (1096), by the Master of the St Lucy Legend, c.1485. *Washington, National Gallery of Art, Samuel H. Kress Collection.*

97. Treble, alto, tenor and bass recorders by Pui Bressan (c.1720). *Chester, Grosvenor Museum.*

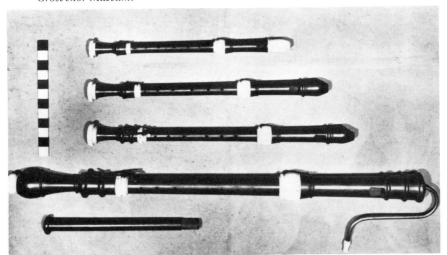

98. Flute played by David in the *Theodore Psalter* of Byzantine origin, dated 1066. *London, British Library, MS. Add. 19352, f.189v.*

wait until the twentieth century to be revived by Arnold Dolmetsch.

The **transverse** or **German flute** (henceforth referred to as 'flute') was certainly known to the Etruscans before the Christian era, and is thought to have originated in Central Asia. It seems to have come to Germany from Byzantium in the twelfth century, but spread only gradually through Europe and with fluctuating success. In France and Flanders its presence was acknowledged by such pictures as those of the *Romance of Alexander* (Oxford, Bodleian Library, MS Bodl. 264, ff.29v., 123, 188v.), illustrated by Jehan de Grise from 1338–44, but after 1400 it was seldom depicted in those parts, presumably due to the popularity of the recorder. It only returned to favour *c.*1500, after which it finally became established also in England, where it was played by the young Henry VIII. His biography by Edward Halle (d.1547) tells how, at 'Wyndsore' in the year 1510–11 he was exercisyng hym selfe daily in shotyng, singing, daunsyng, wrastelyng, casting of the barre, plaiyng at the recorders, flute, virginals, and in settyng of songes, makyng of ballettes, and did set ii. goodly masses, every of them fyve partes, which were song oftentimes in hys chapel, and afterwardes in diverse other places.

The inventory of his instruments in 1547 included flutes made of 'woode', 'glasse', 'woode painted like glasse' and 'iuorie tipped with golde enameled blacke', besides 'phiphes of blacke Ibonie tipped withe Siluer'.

These early flutes were one-piece cylinders, with six fingerholes and no thumb-hole. The 'phiphes', like Virdung's 'Zwerchpfeiff' and Agricola's 'Schweitzerp-feiffen' were early fifes with long, narrow bores, and would normally have been played to the accompaniment of drums. The other flutes are likely to have been wider instruments suitable for consort music, such as the 'Querflöten' of Agricola and Praetorius, who both showed them in three different sizes. Those of Praetorius gave the bottom notes a' (discant), d' (alto or tenor) and g (bass), when their respective six holes were all covered by fingers; the bass flute was built in two sections.

By c.1670 the flute had changed considerably, and probably at the hands of the same craftsmen (Jean Hotteterre and companions) who had altered the recorder. With a natural scale of D (as in the older alto or tenor instrument), it was built in three parts: a cylindrical head joint, a conical body joint, and a small foot joint (either cylindrical or conical) holding a key for the bottom $e\flat'$. The tuning could be remedied to a certain extent by adjusting the length where the parts met, but a more satisfactory method appeared c.1720. This involved the division of the body joint into two sections, the upper of which could be replaced by one of several alternative lengths, known as the *corps de réchange*. Later in the century these themselves became redundant due to the addition of a tuning slide to the foot joint, by which time extra keys had been added to produce a bottom c' and $c\sharp'$. Intonation problems over other chromatic notes were at first remedied by new finger-holes, and later by more keys. Johann Joachim Quantz, whose *Essay of a Method for Playing the Transverse Flute* (1752) is a valuable document on playing and musical style in general, invented an extra key to give the enharmonic change between $e\flat'$ and $d\sharp'$, but it was not widely adopted. Such was the experimentation of the time that by 1800 there were in use flutes with keys ranging in number from one to eight.

The flute had now ousted the recorder for the reason given on page 117. One of its most distinguished exponents was Frederick the Great, who was himself a pupil of Quantz, and his playing was described by Burney after hearing a concert at the emperor's palace of Sans Souci in 1772:

The concert began by a German flute concerto, in which his majesty executed the solo parts with great precision; his *embouchure* was clear and even, his finger brilliant, and his taste pure and simple. I was much pleased, and even surprised with the neatness of his execution in the *allegros*, as well as by his expression and feeling in the *adagio*; in short, his performance surpassed, in many particulars, any thing I had ever heard among *Dilettanti*, or even professors. His majesty played three long and difficult concertos successively, and all with equal perfection.

The nineteenth century saw radical changes aimed at improving tone and intonation, and involving many different mechanisms in which the keys were either 'open' or 'closed' when at rest. A stronger sound than before was produced from the flutes with large fingerholes designed by the Charles Nicholsons, father and son; these were built by T. Prowse from 1822 onwards, and sold by Clementi & Co. of London. Nicholson Junior, himself a virtuoso performer, was heard in 1831 by Theobald Boehm, a goldsmith, jeweller and flautist from Munich, who had already made some very beautiful flutes. Boehm saw the advantage of the large holes, and incorporated them into his design of the following year. This flute, like its immediate predecessor, had a conical body joint, but, due to the elaborate key mechanism, this was now in one piece. Its value was recognized abroad, and from 1843 it was made in London by Rudall and Rose, and in Paris by Clair Godefroy *ainé*. In 1844 Berlioz declared in his *Treatise on Instrumentation* that the flute

for a long time so imperfect in many respects, has now achieved such perfection and evenness of tone that no further improvement remains to be desired.

99.   Flutes, showing the progress made in less than 100 years. From top to bottom, the instruments are made by a) Cahusac, London, *c*.1785; b) Laurent, Paris, early 19th century; c) Clementi & Co., London, *c*.1825 (built by T. Prowse to Nicholson's design); d) Rudall, Rose, Carte & Co., London, 1857–71; e) I. Ziegler, Vienna, *c*.1840 (with a downward extension to g); and f) a Piccolo, late 18th century. *London, Royal College of Music.*

Nevertheless in 1847 Boehm produced a further design, which won a first prize at London's Great Exhibition of 1851. Its chief innovation was the return to a cylindrical body, but with a slightly tapering head, generally described as 'parabolic'. The holes, larger than before, could not be covered by the fingers alone, so were provided with keys in the form of padded lids. The placing of the holes now depended, not on the convenience of the player's fingers, but on acoustic principles. This had already been apparent on the 1832 flute, and had been advocated as early as 1803 by the German flautist Dr H.W. Pottgeisser. Many of Boehm's flutes were from now on made of silver.

Boehm's mechanism necessitated a new fingering system, which discouraged many musicians from adopting it. Hence other designs appeared, some attempting to improve on the old conical eight-keyed flute, and others, such as that of Richard Carte in 1867, combining the best features of the old instrument and of the Boehm flute. This latter is still used by some British flautists, while the 'Reform Flute' by Schwedler of Leipzig (*c.*1885) has been developed until now in Germany. Throughout the western world, however, the Boehm flute is the most played today.

While the normal flute gives c' as its lowest note, various contrivances have managed to extend its range downwards, although still keeping to the basic pitch. Larger flutes have included the alto and tenor sizes in G and F respectively, and basses in C such as the **Albisiphon** created *c.*1911 by Abelardo Albisi of Milan. Of smaller instruments the **fife** represents the continuation of the Renaissance **Schweitzerpfeiff** with its narrow bore, having become smaller through the years and now having its lowest note at bb' or c''. The orchestral piccolo, which generally starts at c'' or d'', was made in three sections with one key in the eighteenth century and later adapted to the Boehm mechanism, but has since reverted to a conical bore. Conical flutes of simple design have long been used in civilian bands.

Reed instruments are much older than transverse flutes, being well documented as far back as the third millennium BC, when a pair of silver pipes was buried in the 'Royal Cemetery' at Ur. A cylindrical pipe with double reed was later termed **aulos** by the Greeks and **tibia** by the Romans. According to *The Learned Banquet* (*Deipnosophistes*) by the 2nd-century (AD) writer Athenaeus of Naucratis,

> there were special *auloi* for each mode, so that at the Games all the *auleti* had to have an *aulos* for each mode.

He added that Pronomius of Thebes (born *c.*475 BC) could play in several modes on one aulos because it had more holes than usual, with ferrules to cover those which were not needed. The aulos or tibia seen most often in the visual arts of Antiquity consisted of two pipes, one accompanying the other, and in the Phrygian version one pipe curved upwards at the end.

In the Middle Ages double reed instruments were occasionally cylindrical but more often conical, and were given the name **calamellus** from *calamus*, a reed. Their English name **shawm** was derived from that of the eastern *zurna*, an instrument said to have terrified the crusaders, and which still survives. In Europe there were three chief ways of arranging the mouthpiece. All of these used a reed fixed onto a staple, which in surviving folk shawms is made of metal. The simplest method was for the staple to be inserted directly into the top end of the instrument in the manner that can be seen in the bagpipe chanter or in the modern Breton *bombarde*. The second way was similar to this but with a flat circular disc loosely fitted round the staple so that the player's lips could rest against it. This survives in many types of eastern *zurna*, and can be seen on a shawm held by an angel on the Minstrels' Gallery at Exeter Cathedral. The third way was a late mediaeval development from the disc principle, involving a shaped wooden block known as the *pirouette*, which held the staple and itself was set into the instrument. In the first two methods the reed usually went right into the performer's mouth and was not controlled by his lips, hence little or no nuance could be obtained. In the third way, however, the lips could exert more control over the reed, thus ensuring some degree of articulation and expression. (A disc can also be called a pirouette.)

From the twelfth century onwards the shawm was often portrayed in art, although at first it was quite short. Then different sizes developed for consort playing, and from the late fourteenth century the instrument was often played in groups of three (described by Tinctoris, *c*.1487, as '*suprema, tenor* – commonly called *bombarde* – and *contra-tenor*'), or with trumpets, sackbuts (trombones), bagpipes or tabors. Large sizes had a key for the lowest note, protected by a *fontanelle*. The word *wait* applied to a shawm or its player when in the context of civic duties, or in the service of the nobility. According to the *Black Book* of his Household, Edward IV had

A WAYTE, that ny3tly, from Mighelmasse til Shere Thursday, pipeth the wache within this court iiij tymes, and in the somer ny3ghtes iij tymes; and he to make bon gayte, and euery chambre dore and office, as well as fyre as for other pikers or perelliz.

Praetorius, who used the word 'Pommer' for any shawm with a key, described sizes from great bass ('bombardone') in *F′* up to the small discant, this latter being the only one to which he actually gave the word 'Schalmeye'. The great bass had four keys, and on the larger sizes of shawm the reed was held in a crook. The word **douçaine**, which appears frequently in mediaeval and Renaissance literature, is thought to have meant a soft reed instrument, possibly with a cylindrical bore.

By this time the French and English terms *hautbois* and *hautboye* were often used for shawms, and some confusion must have arisen when they were also applied to the new oboe. After its arrival the shawm continued in use for many years, gradually becoming used mainly for folk music. One of its latest appearances in art music was as the instrument now known as the **basse de musette**, a very large shawm made in Switzerland during the eighteenth century and often played with church choirs.

100. (Right) Shawm, with a pirouette and double key. Detail from the Flemish painting *Mary Queen of Heaven* (1096), by the Master of the St Lucy Legend, *c*.1485. *Washington, D.C., National Gallery of Art, Samuel H. Kress Collection.*

101.   Oboe, around the base of which are carved scenes of dancers and musicians. Dutch, 17th century. *London, Victoria and Albert Museum.*

For the origins of the **oboe** we look again to the work of Jean Hotteterre the Elder, who came from the village of La Couture-Boussey near Evreux in Normandy. Together with members of the Philidor and Chedeville families, he played in the bands of Louis XIV's *Grande Ecurie*, besides making and repairing instruments for their use. His work on the refined form of bagpipes known as the *musette* must have filled him with a desire to civilize the shawm, and the result appeared in the late 1650s, possibly being played in public for the first time, by Hotteterre himself and Michel Philidor II, in Lully's music for the ballet *L'Amour Malade* in 1657. This new *hautbois* differed from its progenitor in being built in three sections, in having a narrower bore and a narrower reed (with no *pirouette*), and a thumbhole, which had been absent from most shawms. There were three keys, two of them being alternatives for the little finger of either hand, but after *c.*1750 one of these became redundant as most performers played with the left hand above the right. When all the holes and the bottom key were depressed, the lowest note of the oboe was *c′*, while the second key gave *d♯′*. Many instruments had alternative upper joints for adjusting the pitch. In the quest for better intonation the third and fourth holes were doubled to suit enharmonic changes, and extra keys were added towards the end of the eighteenth century by such makers as Grundmann and Grenser of Dresden. Such was the oboe from the time of Lully and Purcell to that of the young Beethoven. In Beethoven's later years, however, the number of keys had increased to 13 in the instruments designed by the Viennese player Josef Sellner and made by Stefan Koch. Their instrument was the basis for

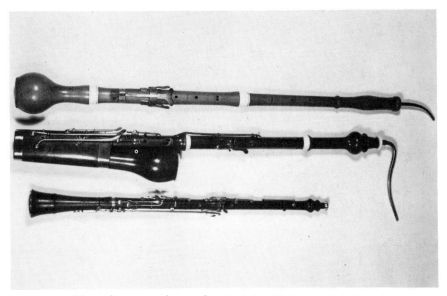

102.   Oboes, from top to bottom by: a) M. Lot, Paris, c.1775–83 (tenor);
b) Triébert, Paris, c.1825 (baritone or bass); c) Tabard, Lyon, c.1835–40.
London, Royal College of Music.

the one played in Germanic countries during the nineteenth century, with only gradual modifications.

In France, however, radical changes were made for refinement. The outline of the oboe became more simple, and the bore was narrowed. One of the first craftsmen to work on adapting the mechanism was Henri Brod (1799–1839), who had studied on a four-keyed oboe and recognized its deficiencies. The German-born Guillaume Triébert (1770–1848) settled in Paris, and with his sons Charles Louis (1810–76) and Frédéric (1813–78) set to work to revise every part of the instrument in successive different 'systems'. Their traditions were later carried on by their foreman François Lorée, whose development of the Triébert 'Système 6' into 'Système A6' became known as the 'Conservatoire model', being used in the classes of Georges Gillet at the Paris Conservatoire from 1882. Among other designers connected to the Triébert firm were Appolon Marie-Rose Barret, whose 1862 mechanism made possible the same fingering for each octave. Independent work was done by Louis Auguste Buffet, who in 1844 patented an oboe adapted to the Boehm mechanism, aided by Boehm himself. With its large holes and large tone it was unacceptable to many French artists, although for a time it was used in military bands. It was, however, further developed by the Parisian P. Soler and the London-based A.J. Lavigne, whose instruments descended to *a*. In the twentieth century the French tradition has been carried on by A. Lorée, while the Austrian oboe has continued, though with less success than before. The German firm of Heckel has welded together the best characteristics of both schools.

103. Oboe by T.W. Howarth, London, 1951, held by its owner Tess Miller of London.

Since the early days of the oboe, other sizes have existed than the treble in C, the nearest being the **oboe d'amore** in A, which flourished during the time of Bach. Tenor oboes in F or G went by such names as **haute-contre de hautbois, taille,** etc., and possibly included

> Deux hautbois de forêt garnis en cuivre, ayant chacun trois corps, qui servent à hausser et baisser le ton, et une petite boette où il y a douze hanches; ils sont de la façon de Bizet

which appeared in an inventory, dated 1780, of instruments in the King's Library at Versailles. (Charles Bizey was a mid-eighteenth-century Parisian oboe-maker.) These may have been some form of **oboe da caccia**, which when called for by

Bach was normally curved, retaining this shape under the name **cor anglais** from the time of Gluck's *Alceste* (1776). Brod made it in a straight form from 1839, although this took time to become established. The bass (baritone) oboe in C often bent back on itself towards the bell, as did some of the tenor instruments. A contra-bass oboe was devised in the late eighteenth century by Delusse of Paris, but had a limited career due to competition from the bassoon. High oboes have been in great demand for military music. An instrument of the oboe family but of very different proportions is the **Heckelphone**, made in 1904 by Wilhelm Heckel in response to a request by Wagner in 1879 for an instrument which 'should combine the character of the oboe with the soft but powerful tones of the Alphorn', the latter being a very long horn traditionally associated with Alpine regions.

During the Renaissance period there appeared several new families of low-pitched double reed instruments. That most resembling the shawm was the **bassanello**, which was said by Praetorius to have been created by Giovanni Bassano of Venice, although this has been disputed by subsequent authorities. In contrast to this long instrument were those of the **rackett** family, also known as **Wurstfagott** (sausage bassoon). The rackett was a short wide cylinder containing cylindrical tubing bent back on itself nine times, and one owned by Praetorius, while only 11 inches deep, descended in sound to C'. A sixteenth-century set of racketts made in the form of dragons can be seen today at the Kunsthistorisches Museum, Vienna. Like the rackett the **sordun** (and its relative the **courtaut**) also had a cylindrical bore, but this was doubled back only once. It was closed at the bottom and gave, according to Praetorius, a sound similar to that of the crumhorn.

104. Cor anglais (English horn) by Carl Golde, Dresden, *c.*1845. *London, Royal College of Music.*

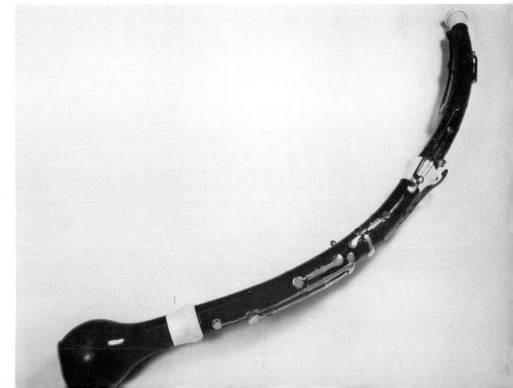

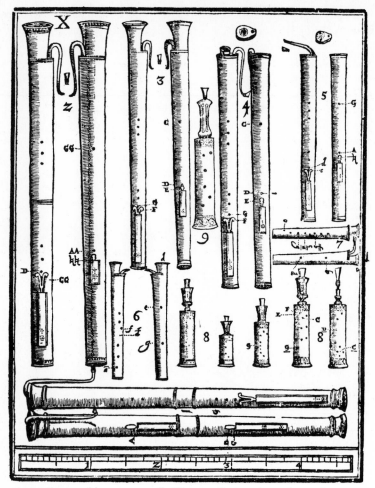

105.   1, Bass sordun; 2–7, curtalls ('Fagotten'); 8, racketts. Praetorius,
Theatrum Instrumentorum (1620), Plate X.

More important because of its historical continuation was the **curtall** (**Dulzian,**
fagotto). Like the sordun it had a double reed on a crook and a bore bent back
once, but this bore was conical. There were two keys. While the lower of the two
sizes of **Doppel-fagotten** went down to F', the most usual size was the **Chorist**
Fagott which was often used in church, and descended to C. By the late seventeenth century the curtall had been divided into four main parts; from the butt
there emerged the tenor ('wing') and bass ('long') joints, and projecting from the
latter the bell which made possible the lowest note Bb'. It is generally assumed
that this change was the work of the Hotteterre circle.

The resulting instrument became known as the **bassoon**, although for a time
the word *curtall* was applied to it, and also *fagotto*, which has never gone out of

106. The Bassoon Player by Harmen Hals (1611–69). This is one of the earliest pictures of the bassoon after it had developed from the curtal. *Aachen, Suermondt Museum.*

use. Early bassoons had much wider reeds than those of today, and in instruments by Johann Cristoph Denner (1655–1707), his son Jacob (d.1735), and their contemporaries, there were three keys. A fourth had appeared before 1750, and it was for such an instrument that Mozart wrote his *Bassoon Concerto* in 1774. By 1800 there were six keys, but in spite of very good instruments by Grundmann and members of the Grenser family, it was not possible to play smoothly in all tonalities. This problem was tackled by Carl Almenräder, who produced a 15-keyed bassoon c.1820, but at the expense of its tone. From 1831 he worked in partnership with Johann Adam Heckel, whose son Wilhelm considerably widened the bore. Successive members of the family have continued the business, and the firm of Heckel now produces some of the best bassoons in the world. Boehm

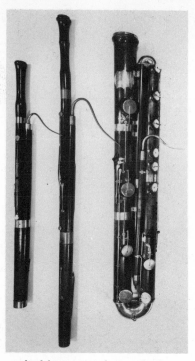

107. Bassoons, from left to right: a) (?) English, late 18th century; b) Quart-bassoon marked '2/Samme/London', *c.*1853; c) Contra-bassophon by Alfred Morton, London, *c.*1876. *London, Royal College of Music.*

108. (Right) Contrebasse à anche; French, late 19th century. *London, Horniman Museum.*

109. (Far right) Crumhorns and timbrel, in an intarsia panel by Fra Giovanni Barile, 1513–21. *Rome, Vatican, Stanza della Segnatura.*

applied his principles to the bassoon with the help of F. Triébert, producing an instrument which won a prize at the London Exhibition of 1862, although its vast cost prevented it from being widely adopted. The best French bassoons of today are by the firm of Buffet-Crampon at Paris, according to Anthony Baines (*Woodwind Instruments and their History*), who, in comparing the relative merits of the German and French bassoons, wrote that while the French instrument is 'more subtle and vocal', the Heckel bassoon is 'more uniformly effective in the orchestra'. Professor Giles Brindley's electrified **Logical Bassoon** is mentioned on page 188.

During its history the different sizes of bassoon have included the **tenoroon**, pitched a fourth or fifth higher than the usual instrument, and the **contrabassoon** (double bassoon) descending to *B* ''. On 6 August 1739 the *London Daily Post and General Advertiser* announced that in Marylebone Gardens, London, there would be played.

Two Grand or Double Bassoons, made by Mr. Stanesby, jun. the Greatness of whose sound surpasses that of any other Base Instrument whatsoever. Never performed before.

A shorter and more bulky instrument was the **Contrabassophon**, invented by H.J. Haseneier of Coblenz in 1847. It was played a good deal in England, and appeared in the Handel Festival of 1871.

Related to the oboe and bassoon is the likewise conically-bored **Sarrusophone**,

which was created by the French bandmaster Sarrus and patented by P.L. Gautrot of Paris in 1856. Made of brass and with a double reed, its smaller sizes (now obsolete) were straight, while the larger ones somewhat resembled the bassoon and contrabassoon in shape. Like the saxophone, which inspired it, the sarrusophone has been used to a great extent in military bands, as have other double-reed brass instruments such as the **contrebasse-à-anche**, which was played mainly on the Continent during the latter part of the nineteenth century.

During the Middle Ages certain pipes were fitted with a bladder which acted as an air reservoir above the double reed. Today they are called **bladder-pipes**. In the late fifteenth century there emerged a new class of instruments which had no bladder, but the reed was covered by a wooden cap containing a narrow mouth-hole. The most spectacular of these was the cylindrically-bored **crumhorn** which curved, horn-like, at its lower end, and was a popular consort instrument for about 150 years. Other reed-cap instruments included the conical **Rauschpfeife**, which was virtually a covered shawm, the **corna muse** which appeared to be straight and was covered below, producing a soft sound, and the similar-looking **Schryari** or **Schreierpfeiffen** which, by having their ends uncovered, sounded, according to Praetorius, 'strong and fresh in tone'. An inventory taken at the castle of Cassel on 24 February 1613 included four different sizes of Schryari besides '1 *Krumbhorn* case with 8 Krumbhörner of different sizes', and a *Strach*, described there as a 'long straight instrument, basset to the *Krumbhörner*'.

Instruments with only a single reed came late to European art music, although in primitive forms they had been known from Antiquity. In the mediaeval **hornpipe**

(surviving later as a folk instrument) they were combined with an expanding bell of horn, and later made a short appearance in the **Phagotum** invented by Canon Afranio of Ferrara (1480–*c.*1565). It is significant that they were mentioned neither by Praetorius nor by Mersenne.

In the late seventeenth century, however, a new instrument called the **chalumeau** came onto the musical scene. (The name, incidentally, had already been used for the shawm.) This was a cylindrical pipe with seven fingerholes, a thumbhole, sometimes one or two keys, and a single beating reed fixed to the upper side of the mouthpiece. Its disadvantage lay in its range of less than one and a half octaves, and it could not overblow.

This problem was solved *c.*1700 by Johann Christoph Denner of Nuremberg, and in doing so he created the **clarinet**. By altering the position and size of the keyed holes, he made playable the third and fifth harmonics, sounding a twelfth and eighteenth respectively above the fundamental. (When the reed is held between the player's lips the clarinet acts as a stopped pipe, and as such cannot sound harmonics at the octave. The subsequent development of the instrument was aimed at making playable all the notes between the bottom and top, and on smoothing out as far as possible their difference of tone.) Apart from their single reed and two keys, Denner's clarinets looked very much like treble recorders, and were built in three parts. Gradually new keys were added to fill in the missing notes, so that by the time of Mozart's maturity there were five, and by 1790 there were six. (Because of the difficulties of fingering, clarinets were made as transposing instruments in different pitches.) The instrument was now fully chromatic, but the notes were of uneven quality. This was considerably remedied by the Russian-born Ivan Müller who, *c.*1812, made a 13-keyed clarinet with improved intonation due to its holes being placed more correctly than before. His fingering system enabled performance in any key, and he claimed that alternative instruments were no longer necessary. Among other makers to facilitate awkward jumps was Adolphe Sax of Brussels, who also extended the range of pitch downwards.

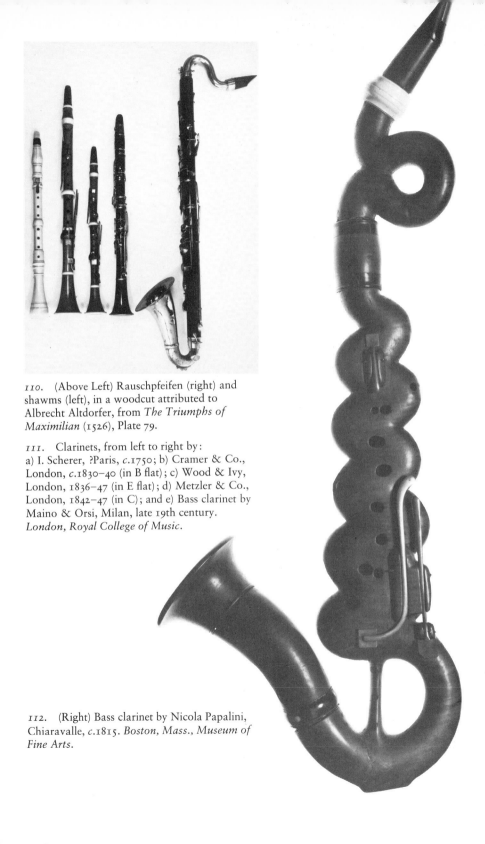

110. (Above Left) Rauschpfeifen (right) and shawms (left), in a woodcut attributed to Albrecht Altdorfer, from *The Triumphs of Maximilian* (1526), Plate 79.

111. Clarinets, from left to right by: a) I. Scherer, ?Paris, *c.*1750; b) Cramer & Co., London, *c.*1830–40 (in B flat); c) Wood & Ivy, London, 1836–47 (in E flat); d) Metzler & Co., London, 1842–47 (in C); and e) Bass clarinet by Maino & Orsi, Milan, late 19th century. *London, Royal College of Music.*

112. (Right) Bass clarinet by Nicola Papalini, Chiaravalle, *c.*1815. *Boston, Mass., Museum of Fine Arts.*

Inevitably there appeared a 'Boehm clarinet', although Boehm himself was not involved with its production. This was the work of Hyacinthe Klosé and Auguste Buffet between 1839 and 1843. With further attention to the position of holes, to the type of their keys, and to economy of fingering, they devised the clarinet which is among the most used in America and western Europe today. Many professional clarinettists still like to use alternative instruments in A and B flat, which, with their downward extensions, actually sound *c♯* and *d* for their lowest notes.

Larger instruments included the late eighteenth-century **clarinette d'amour**, which had its mouthpiece attached to a crook, and was distinguished by a bulbous bell; it was succeeded by the **alto clarinet** in F or E flat around 1820. The **bass clarinet** has been designed in very varied ways, resembling a curtall or bassoon *c.*1800, and appearing in a snake-like form in Italy about ten years later. Adolphe Sax made straight ones (*c.*1845) with the bell facing downwards in contrast to its previous position, but more recent designs have turned it upwards again. Many designs have appeared for a **contrabass clarinet**, notably the **Bathyphon** patented by W. Wieprecht and E. Skorra of Berlin in 1839, the **Pedal Clarinet** of Fontaine-Besson of Paris in 1889, and current models by the firms of Selmer and Buffet.

Of earlier vintage was the **basset horn**, attributed to A. and M. Mayrhofer of Passau, *c.*1770. Its early shape was curved, then angular, and later on straight, its distinguishing feature being a 'box' in which the tubing doubled back on itself to save the overall length; its lowest note was F. The composers with which it is chiefly associated are Mozart, Mendelssohn and Richard Strauss, and between

113. (Far left) Basset horn, of a type used in the music of Mozart; probably Viennese, *c.*1780. *Nuremberg, Germanisches Nationalmuseum.*

114. (Left) Saxophone, in its recent 'Mark 7' tenor model by H. Selmer, Paris, 1976.

115. (Right) Bagpipes and shawm, played for a banquet of the Order of the Star. Detail from the *Grandes Chroniques de France*, French, 14th century. *Paris, Bibliothèque Nationale, MS Fr. 2813, f.394.*

their eras it was used to a considerable extent in military bands. Berlioz, in his suggestions for 'the finest concert orchestra', suggested the use of 'one basset-horn or one bass clarinet'.

In the nineteenth century there appeared several single-reed instruments with a conical bore. The most important is the **saxophone**, invented by Adolphe Sax *c.*1842; it occurs in various sizes of which the smallest are straight and the largest have an upturned bell and crook. It has been used to a considerable extent in military and jazz bands, and for occasional special effects in orchestral music. A wooden relative is the **tarogato**, originally a double-reed folk instrument from Hungary, but later adapted for a single-reed mouthpiece, and called for in the final act of Wagner's *Tristan*.

Last but not least come the **bagpipes**, which combine characteristics of all the reed instruments mentioned above. In the *Orationes* of Dio Chrysostom (born *c.*40 AD) we are told that the Emperor Nero could 'play the pipes, both by means of his lips and by tucking a skin beneath his armpits'. From this time onwards information about the bagpipes is scanty, and it is not until the Middle Ages that their history becomes more clear. In the 9th-century letter from 'Jerome' to 'Dardanus' (see page 27) one interpretation of the word 'chorus' is of a bag from which project a mouthpipe and a chanter. This is illustrated in the many manuscripts containing the letter, and from the twelfth century the instrument appears in independent sources, one example being a carving at the Spanish abbey of Ripoll. While this simple bagpipe continued in use for some time, the most usual mediaeval type had appeared by 1250. This had the bag, mouthpipe and chanter

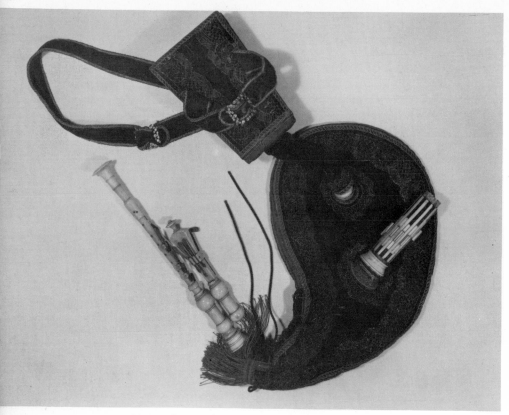

116.   Musette from 18th-century France. *London, Royal College of Music.*

as before, but also a drone pipe, which became one of the most important characteristics of the instrument. Although the *Cantigas de Santa Maria* manuscript
shows a bagpipe with four drones, these are exceptional, and it was not until the
fifteenth century that two or more drone pipes became frequent. Bellows were
applied to Irish bagpipes before 1600, and have since been used in the French
musette, the Northumbrian small-pipe, and the Bohemian *dudy*, to name but a
few. The **musette**, which was played by the artificially rustic French nobility
during the reign of Louis XIV and later, and was improved by Jean Hotteterre the
Elder, had two ivory or ebony cylindrical chanters with silver keys, and a cylinder
containing four interchangeable drones; moreover, all its reeds were double. The
bagpipes best known today are perhaps those of Scotland, which in their large
type have a mouthpipe, chanter and three drones, but numerous other varieties
can be found as folk instruments in different parts of Europe.

The role of the bagpipe in history has been one of the most varied among
instruments. A favourite for shepherds to play while guarding their sheep, it has
also been played to accompany such activities as dancing, acrobatics, and

117.   Bagpipers of the Argyll and Sutherland Highlanders at the Military Exhibition, 1890.

tournaments, and processions for weddings, funerals and pilgrimages, besides amusing the *dilettante* noblemen mentioned above. From the Middle Ages onwards it has been used for military purposes, and today massed bands of pipers play to the world during the Edinburgh International Festival. An instrument of great importance in its own right, it has remained outside the confines of the symphony orchestra, except in such rare cases as the *Peasant Wedding* (1755) by Leopold Mozart.

— CHAPTER VI —

The Brass Families

The 'brass' instruments, like those of the 'woodwind' families, have during their history been made from a great variety of materials. In all cases their sound is generated by the vibrating lips of the player, often against a cup-shaped mouth-piece. Allowing for many hybrids, they can broadly be divided into two types: those with a conical bore comprising horns, and those with a cylindrical bore, namely trumpets.

From the earliest sound-producing horns, those of animals, there emerged two main lines of descent. One consisted of instruments on which could be played only notes from the harmonic series (though later on valves permitted all notes of the scale to be sounded), while the other comprised those with fingerholes. Due to their close connection with the woodwind instruments, this latter group will be considered first.

Because the simple animal horn was incapable of sounding adjacent notes,

118. Horn with fingerholes, from a Book of Hours made in Milan, *c.*1494, for the Sforza family. *London, British Library, MS Add. 34294, f.34v.*

fingerholes were added to it at an early date, and from the Romanesque period onwards it was often depicted thus in the hands of shepherds. It was later imitated in wood and became an instrument of art music with the name **cornett** (Italian **cornetto**; German **Zinck**), being already known in this form before 1400. Many examples have survived from the sixteenth century onwards, some being of wood covered with leather, and others being of ivory; its sizes were treble, tenor and bass, with an occasional high **cornettino**. While some were straight, most were curved, and the exotic snake-like shape of the larger ones avoided too great a distance between the fingerholes. During the Renaissance and early Baroque periods, cornetts were frequently played with church choirs, as they sounded not unlike the human voice. Their popularity eventually waned with the ascendancy of the oboe.

119. 1–4, Trombones; 5–9 cornetts, straight and curved; 10, trumpet; 11, hunting trumpet; 12, wooden trumpet; 13, trumpet crook. Praetorius, *Theatrum Instrumentorum* (1620), Plate VIII.

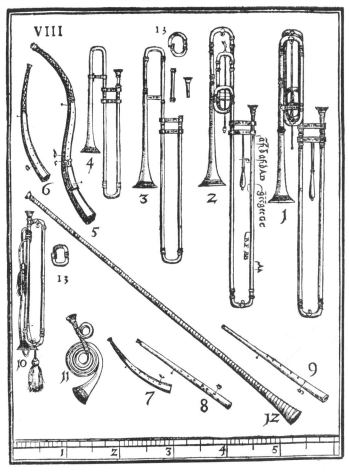

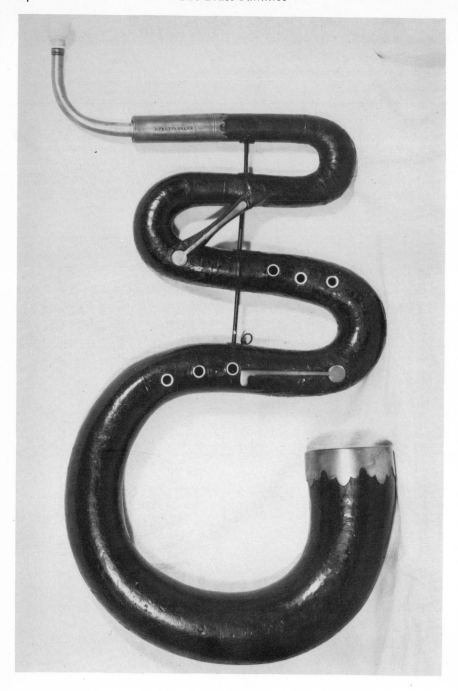

120. Serpent, by Francis Pretty, Lambeth, after 1838. *London, Royal College of Music.*

Somewhat similar to the bass cornett, but with a much wider conical bore and thinner walls, was the **serpent**, which according to the Abbé Leboeuf (*Mémoire concernant l'histoire ecclésiastique et civile d'Auxerre*, Paris, 1743), was invented by Canon Edmé Guillaume of Auxerre in about 1590. Early examples had just six fingerholes, but up to 14 keys were added after 1800. One of its chief uses was described by Burney during his French tour of 1770:

> In the French churches there is an instrument on each side of the choir, called the serpent, from its shape, I suppose, for it undulates like one. This gives the *tone* in chanting, and plays the base when they sing in parts. It is often ill-played, but if judiciously used, would have a good effect. It is, however, in general overblown, and too powerful for the voices it accompanies; otherwise, it mixes with them better than the organ, as it can augment or diminish a sound with more delicacy, and is less likely to overpower or destroy by a bad temperament, that perfect one, of which the voice only is capable.

The serpent was also used in military bands and in orchestras, either in its own right or as a substitute for the bassoon family, as happened when it deputized for the double bassoon in a performance at the Paris Opéra of Haydn's *Creation* in 1800. Although it gave way to the ophicleide after *c.*1830, it was still widely used later in the century. Related instruments were the V-shaped copper or brass **bass horn**, and the wooden **Russian bassoon**, which had a dragon's-head bell. Both these instruments flourished in similar conditions to the serpent in the nineteenth century.

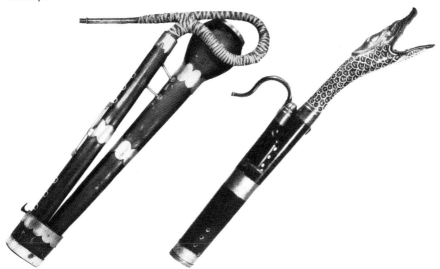

121.   Bass horn, possibly by Astor, London, early 19th century. *London, Horniman Museum.*

122.   (Right) Russian bassoon by Jeantet, Lyon, *c.*1825. *London, Horniman Museum.*

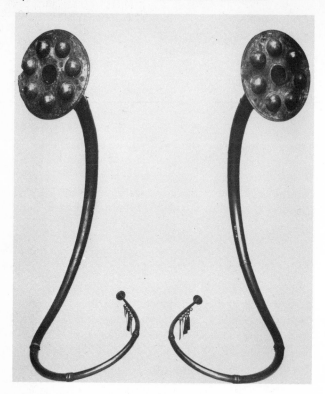

123. Lurs from the
Bronze Age, discovered
at Brudevaelte Moor,
North Sealand,
Denmark. *Copenhagen,
Danish National
Museum.*

124. (Right) Horn in
its most simple form,
from a margin of the
Luttrell Psalter, made in
England *c.*1335–40.
*London, British Library,
MS. Add 42130, f.43v.*

Simple horns without fingerholes, and with the mouthpiece carved out of the body itself, go back to remote Antiquity. Some were used mainly for outdoor signalling, while others, such as the Jewish **shofar** (a ram or goat horn), had ritual purposes. Long before the advent of Christianity, however, they had inspired the making of metal horns, perhaps the most spectacular being the Bronze Age **lurs** which have been discovered in Scandinavian peat bogs. These bronze instruments were played in pairs, each of the two being tuned to the same basic note, and they were capable of producing a wide range of natural sounds. Their flat disc at the wide end is seen to a lesser extent in horns of about the same period excavated in Ireland. The almost circular Roman **cornu** (see plate 73), which was often played with the tuba and the hydraulis, was held in such a way that its bell was in the uppermost position, high above the player's shoulder. The Roman **buccina** has not yet been sufficiently identified, but it seems to have been some kind of horn. Anthony Baines (*Brass Instruments*, pp. 68–69) has suggested that the Byzantine **boukina** may have been the 'cavalry salpinx' of 'leather and thin wood' which, according to Procopius (*The History of the Wars* VI, xxiii) was used in the army of Belisarius in 540.

In the Dark Ages and the early mediaeval period, animal horns were again the most used in Europe, the most distinguished of them being the carved ivory **oliphant** which came from Byzantium and was used in battle by warriors. Larger

horns of metal were again widespread by the late fourteenth century, being well represented on a misericord of that time in Worcester Cathedral, where a huntsman's horn bends round his body. A vivid description of one of the mediaeval uses of horns is given in Froissart's *Chronicles*:

> The Scots infantry all carry horns slung on their shoulders, in the manner of hunters. The horns are all of different sizes, and when they are all blown together, in different keys, they can be heard four miles away by day, and six miles away by night, to the terror and consternation of their enemies, and the great delight of themselves . . . the noise was as if all the devils in hell had gathered together.

It was for hunting and military purposes that horns were mainly used for the next 300 years, with their shapes varying from straight to any degree of curvature. Tightly-coiled horns lasted from the fifteenth century to the early twentieth, but it was the large seventeenth-century horn with one or two coils which led to the orchestral **French horn** of today. Wide enough to carry over the shoulder, some of its best surviving examples are by the Crétien family of Vernon in Normandy. Horn music was played by a string orchestra in Cavalli's opera *Le Nozze di Teti e di Peleo* (1639), and from the time of Lully's ballet *La Princesse d'Elide* (1664), horns themselves were increasingly used for fanfare effects in dramatic performances. Franz Anton, Count von Sporck, heard such hunting horns at the court of Louis XIV, and introduced them to Bohemia on his return there in 1681. Soon afterwards they were known in Vienna.

Michael Leichnambschneider of Austria seems to have been responsible for turning the horn into a truly orchestral instrument, by the addition of crooks not later than 1703, and by reducing its size to create a more sonorous sound. These were coils of different lengths which, when added to the main tube, lengthened it and therefore lowered the basic pitch, although not increasing the number of available notes. All orchestral horn music up to c.1750 was therefore theoretically restricted to notes of the harmonic series, although in practice the lower harmonics could be lowered still further in pitch by the 'falset' technique of relaxing the embouchure.

In the mid eighteenth century horn-playing was revolutionized by hand-stopping, in which notes other than the natural harmonics could be produced by the performer inserting his hand into the bell of the instrument, to a greater or lesser degree. This meant that a complete scale was now available, although with a difference of *timbre* between the natural and stopped notes. To accommodate the hand, the position of the horn was adapted so that the bell pointed downwards. A player much associated with this technique, even if he did not invent it, was the Bohemian-born Anton Joseph Hampl, who worked in Dresden. From his time, at least until that of Brahms, composers wrote for the handhorn, which itself went through several modifications. In the earliest surviving crooked horns (dating from the mid eighteenth century) one or more crooks were added between the main body of the instrument and the master crook, which held the mouthpiece.

125. Two horns played with handhorn technique, two violins, viola and bass, on the title page of Mozart's *A Musical Joke*, K.522, published posthumously in 1801. *London, British Library, Hirsch IV. 128.*

According to the number of crooks added, the bell was at a different distance from the player's mouth. This was inconvenient for hand-stopping, so around 1753 Hampl devised a new system by which the crooks were added at the centre of the instrument and the mouthpiece remained at the same distance from the hand. The resulting **Inventionshorn** was first made by Johann Werner of Dresden, and later by Johann Gottfried Haltenhof of Hanau-am-Mayn, whose instruments contained a tuning slide for adjusting the pitch to that of other instruments. A strengthened type of Inventionshorn was the *Cor Solo*, designed by Joseph Raoux of Paris, *c.*1780, especially for the use of virtuosi. This had crooks for G F E E♭ and D, the keys most needed for solo horn music. Orchestral horns, however, needed at least nine crooks, and so, to avoid the inconvenience of carrying them all around, there appeared **Omnitonic horns**, of which the earliest surviving example is by J.-B. Dupont of Paris, and dates from about 1815. This instrument is now kept at the Paris Conservatoire. Its basic principle is that detachable crooks are replaced by the necessary amount of tubing built into the main instrument, the correct amount for each fundamental pitch being opened up by a device which varied from one instrument to another. The technique of handstopping, however, still needed to be used. Other methods of dispensing with detachable crooks had included the

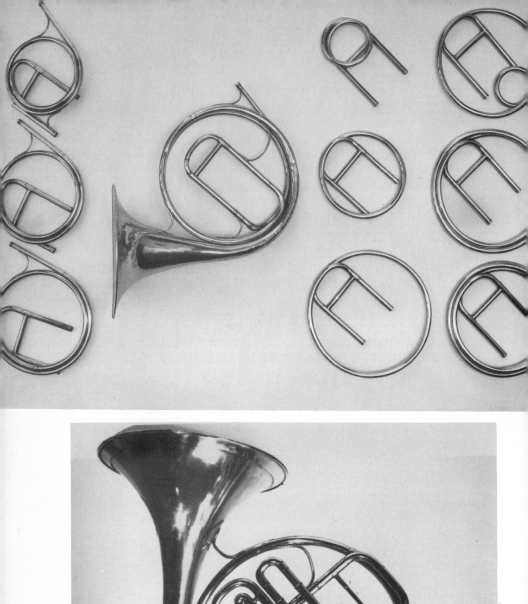

short-lived **Amor-schall**, invented about 1766 by the Bohemian Kölbel who worked in St Petersburg. No example of this instrument is known to survive, but it is said to have had keys and a bulbous bell, to which was attached another bulbous shape containing small holes.

Of more lasting importance was the **valve horn**, foreshadowed as far back as 1788, when the Irishman Charles Clagget invented the 'Cromatic Trumpet and French Horn', but these disappeared after a few performances. In Berlin in 1818 Heinrich Stölzel of Saxony and Friedrich Blühmel of Silesia patented the use of valves, bringing together their own discoveries, of which Stölzel's part had already been publicized in 1815. Their horns were furnished with two piston valves, each of which made available a greater length of tubing; the pitch accordingly descended a semitone or tone as required. In the 1830s a third piston was added, which lowered the pitch by yet another semitone. Since then many types of valve have been invented, but those most used today are the rotary valve, apparently invented by Joseph Riedl of Vienna in c.1832, and the type of piston valve produced by François Périnet of Paris in 1839. In fact the valve horn was not widely used at first, as players and listeners preferred the sound of the natural horn, which was used until late in the century. The great advantage of the valve horn, however, was that the changes previously made by removing crooks between playing could now be effected during performance, and the instrument was chromatic within itself. While the basic pitch of the horn has varied much during its history, it is nowadays a transposing instrument normally in F, or, in the double horn, adaptable from F to B flat.

The principle of adding keys to brass instruments was applied to the singly-coiled copper **bugle horn** and patented by Joseph Halliday of Dublin in 1810. This **keyed bugle** in C or B flat was very popular until the middle of the century,

126.   (Above left) Inventionshorn with its crooks, by Gustav Pfretzschner, Neukirchen, c.1840. *Copenhagen, Musikhistorisk Museum.*

127.   (Left) French horn with valves; 19th century, *London, Horniman Museum.*

128.   Keyed bugle by Greenhill, London, 1824–29. *London, Royal College of Music.*

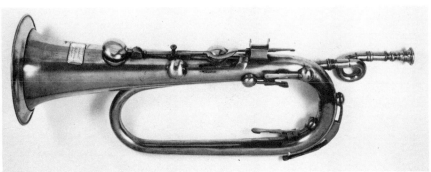

particularly in Britain and America. A larger form, the **ophicleide,** was invented by Halary of Paris in 1817 (patented in 1821) and made of brass, somewhat resembling a bassoon in shape. The most usual size, pitched in C or B flat, was frequently used as a bass to the brass instruments of the orchestra, only becoming obsolete with the final acceptance of the orchestral tuba. Both the keyed bugle and the ophicleide were prominent in military music, and the ophicleide appears in a photograph of the Crediton Town Band taken in 1862 by William Hector (plate 201).

The introduction of valves reformed not only the French horn, but also some of its minor relatives. The bugle with valves was known as the **flugel horn,** while the valved circular **posthorn** became the **cornet-à-pistons** *c.*1827 in the hands of

129. (Right) Bass ophicleide, on the title page of *Solfège-Méthode pour l'Ophicléide Basse*, by V. Caussinus, Paris, *c*.1840. *London, British Library, h.2295.a.*

130. (Left) Cornet-à-pistons by Guichard, Breveté, Paris, before 1845. *London, Horniman Museum.*

131. Orchestral tuba in F, made by Boosey & Hawkes in 1955 for Gerard Hoffnung, who is seen playing it here.

Halary, its English name first being **cornopean**. There are many other 'horns', united by their conical bore and use of valves, but of very varying shapes and sizes, and confusing terminology. These include instruments going by the names of **euphonium, bombardon, alto, tenor, baritone** and **bass (tuba) horns**, and the family of **saxhorns**, patented by Adolphe Sax in 1845. Their main use is in brass band music. Of the **tuba** family, the most important is the **bass tuba** in F, patented by Wieprecht and J.G. Moritz of Berlin in 1835, which eventually superseded the serpent, bass horn, Russian bassoon and ophicleide. The lowest tuba is the **subcontrabass** in B flat. Wagner's special 'tubas' designed for *The Ring* have occasionally been used by other composers, notably Richard Strauss. Related to the tuba are the circular **helicon**, associated with Wieprecht and Stowasser, *c.*1849, and a somewhat similar instrument with a very long bell which was invented by John Philip Sousa and in 1908 became adopted by American army bands under the name **Sousaphone**.

In contrast to the horn, the **trumpet** family normally has a cylindrical bore. Up to the Middle Ages, however, this was often conical, the character of the instrument appearing in its straight outline and expanding bell. It is well documented in ancient arts, and surviving specimens include two from the tomb of Tutankhamun who reigned in Egypt from *c.*1361–1352 BC; one of these is of bronze and gold, and the other is of silver. The Greek **salpinx** and the Roman **tuba** were long trumpets, mainly cylindrical and with a flared bell. The Roman **lituus**, on the other hand, had a curved bell, at first being made from a reed pipe terminating in a horn, and later being fashioned in bronze.

With the collapse of the Roman Empire the trumpet, like the organ, disappeared from most of Europe, and is next seen on a wide scale in the visual arts of the Middle Ages. Early examples are in the French 9th-century Apocalypse at Trier (Stadtbibliothek MS 31), and in a fresco of the Cathedral Baptistery at Novara, dating from *c.*1000. From this time onwards the metal trumpet gradually spread again through Europe, its distinctive pommels (bosses) and cylindrical bore becoming established through eastern influence at about the time of the Third Crusade. Such instruments, however, are not normally seen in English art until after 1200, their predecessors being long, straight and conical instruments very probably made of wood, as seen in the British Museum MS Cotton Tib.C.vi, f.18v., of *c.*1050. Nevertheless even these are rare in English sources of the time, and most contemporary illustrations of the word *tuba* (as in the Apocalypse) show an unmistakably curved horn.

Once it had become established, the true trumpet became one of the most important instruments, on account of its use on ceremonial occasions, whether of peace or of war. While the names **trumpe** and **buisine** were often used for long trumpets, **trompette** and **clarion** for shorter ones, and **beme** possibly for wooden ones, the matter has been considerably confused by poetic licence. Of certain value, however, is Maurice Byrne's discovery, in documents of the Goldsmiths' Company, that in 1391 certain specified 'trompes' weighed more than 'clarions' (*GSJ* XXIV, 1971, 63). The following excerpts show some of the ways in which these instruments fitted into society.

132. Two trumpets and nakers, played at a feast. Detail from an enamelled cruet made in Paris in 1333. *Copenhagen, Danish National Museum.*

A barge shall mete you full right
With four and twenty ores full bright
With trompettes and with clarioune
The freshe water to rowe up and doune.

(Anon., *The Squire of Low Degree*, c.1450, l.811–814.)

Tho saugh I in an other place
Stonden in a large space,
Of hem that maken blody soun
In trumpe, beme, and claryoun;
For in fight and blod-shedynge
Ys used gladly clarionynge.

(Chaucer, *The House of Fame*, c.1375, l.1237–1242.)

By the mid fourteenth century trumpets had become so long that some of them were bent back into a shape like a flattened letter S. These and the straight ones were often played together, a striking example being in a picture of the Battle of Agincourt (1415) from the St Albans Chronicle (London, Lambeth Palace, MS 6, f.243). About this time the instrument was also looped right over, in the form later described by Virdung as 'Clareta'.

133. 'Clareta' and 'Thurner Horn' from Virdung's *Musica Getutscht* (1511). Both may have been slide trumpets, and the latter is known to have been played frequently on towers.

134. Trumpet made by William Bull of London in the late 17th century. *London, Museum of London.*

While the straight form remained for heraldic purposes, folded trumpets became normal, generally pitched in D. Praetorius, however, said that

a short time ago it became the practice in many court orchestras either to use the trumpet in a lengthened form or to attach crook tubes to its front

to bring it down to C. On it the harmonic series was divided into two main registers, the *principale* (medium) and *clarino* (upper), with different players specializing in each, although there was no difference in the instruments themselves. Clarino playing, which uses the adjacent notes of the harmonic series, was used by Monteverdi in *Orfeo* (1607) and reached its zenith in the time of Bach, who immortalized it in his *Second Brandenburg Concerto* (1721). Later in the eighteenth century this high register was abandoned, and the trumpet was again used mainly for music of a fanfare type, whether in or out of the orchestra. It was now pitched in F or E flat. An invaluable guide to eighteenth-century trumpets, with their history, technique and social standing, can be found in the *Trumpeters' and Kettledrummers' Art* by Johann Ernst Altenburg, published at Halle in 1795.

The trumpet described so far, whether straight, folded, or sometimes even coiled, had produced the natural harmonics in whatever key it was built (or crooked). One of the first attempts to make it chromatic came in the Renaissance **slide trumpet**, in which the mouthpiece was fixed to a movable piece of tube. The player would hold this in one hand close to his mouth, and with the other pull the rest of the instrument further away, lowering the basic pitch possibly by as much as a perfect fourth. By this means the trumpet could play a wide range of chromatic notes, and was able to play with voices and other instruments in Renaissance polyphony, which the normal trumpet could hardly do. A surviving Baroque **Zugtrompete** by Hans Veit of Naumberg, dated 1651 (now in the Institut fur Musikforschung, Berlin), is thought to have been the type of instrument specified by Bach as the 'tromba da tirarsi'. In the late seventeenth century an English variety was known as the **flat trumpet** because it could play the 'flat' notes involved in minor keys. At the funeral solemnity of Queen Mary in 1694 a Full Anthem by Purcell was 'accompanied with flat Mournfull Trumpets', according to the British Library MS Harl. 7340, f.521. This instrument, which was described in detail by James Talbot between 1685 and 1701, was the predecessor of the English slide trumpet (normally in F) much associated with John Hyde in the late eighteenth century, and which lasted about 100 years. The French also made slide trumpets to a limited degree at this time.

Further attempts to make the chromatic notes playable included the **Stopftrompete** or **Trompette demilune** of the eighteenth and early nineteenth centuries, using handstopping techniques which, however, proved less successful than on the horn. Its French name came from the curved shape in which not only the main body, but also the crooks were built. A **keyed trumpet**, such as that by Joseph Riedl which was being played by the Viennese Anton Weidinger in 1801, is thought to have been the instrument for which Haydn wrote his *Trumpet Concerto* in 1796.

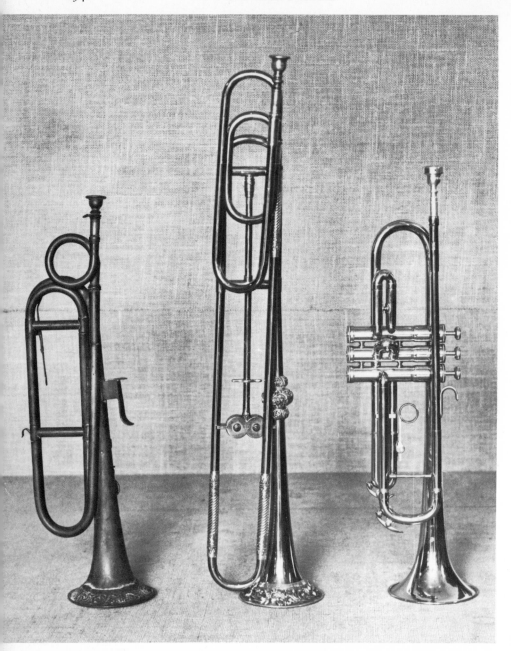

135.   Trumpets, from left to right: a) Keyed trumpet (with mouthpiece missing) by W. Sandbach, London, 1812; b) Slide trumpet by I. Kohler, London, 1860; c) Valve trumpet by Conn, U.S.A., 1976. *London, Royal Military School of Music, Kneller Hall.* (The valve trumpet is owned by Bandsman J. Mitchell.)

Mechanization of the trumpet, which can be traced back to Charles Clagget's invention of 1788 (see page 147), became permanent with the invention of valves, but only after they had been applied to the horn. Early references to **valve trumpets** include Wieprecht's use of them in a Prussian band in 1824, and Spontini's despatching of some from Germany to Paris two years later. For a long time, however, the natural trumpet was used unless the valve one was specified, and in England the slide trumpet was considered adequate for most of the century. The basic pitch varied considerably, that of F being the most usual in orchestral circles until *c*.1910, since when it has been replaced by C or B flat, although alternatives are still available.

As the art of clarino playing had vanished before 1800, the modern revival of Baroque music has caused experiments to find a **'Bach' trumpet**. One of the first was produced by Julius Kosleck, who played it for Bach's Bicentenary in 1885; it consisted of a long buisine-like instrument with two valves. After further valve-trumpet attempts by C. Mahillon & Co. of Brussels in 1892, Werner Menke of Leipzig *c*.1934, and others, a new natural form described as **clarino** was produced in 1959 by Otto Steinkopf and Helmut Finke, based on a coiled trumpet of post-horn shape in a portrait of Bach's Leipzig trumpeter Gottfried Reiche (d.1734).

In the fifteenth century the folded slide trumpet was adapted so that, instead of having a single movable tube with mouthpiece attached (although this type continued to be used), it had a two-legged slide which extended the back part of the instrument. This was the point at which the **trombone** developed from the trumpet, and it was to follow a very different path. The Italian word *trombone* was already in use before 1460, but the English and French preferred to call the instrument by some form of the word **sackbut**, and to the Germans it was **Posaune**. According to Edward Halle's *King Henry VIII*, when that monarch entertained the Emperor Charles V in London in 1522,

> . . . they passed to the Conduite in Cornehill where the strete was enclosed from side to side with ii gates to open and shitte, and over the gates wer arches with towers embattailed set with vanes and scutchions of the armes of the Emperor and the kyng, and over the arches were two towers, the one full of Trompettes and the other full of Shalmes and shagbuttes whiche played continually. . . .

It is not known where the trombone originated, but the earliest recorded maker of them was Hans Neuschel II of Nuremberg, a town celebrated for its brass instruments. Neuschel made instruments for Maximilian I, and his portrait appears in *The Triumphs of Maximilian* (1526) at the express wish of the emperor himself, whose instructions had already been given in 1512. A tenor trombone by Georg Neuschel, the son of Hans II, is dated 1557, and now belongs to Dr René Clemencic of Vienna.

Like many other Renaissance and Baroque instruments, trombones were built in different sizes. Four were known to Praetorius, namely the **alto, tenor, bass** and **contrabass**, and a **soprano** was also used in the eighteenth century. The tenor

in B flat was, and still is, the instrument most used, descending normally to *E*, while the **contrabass** was an octave lower. Praetorius said that with careful playing it could be made to go lower still, and was sometimes supplied with crooks for that purpose, as were the other sizes. Chromatic music was no problem as trombones could play with the slide in seven different positions. During this early period these instruments were used to a great extent in church music, particularly in association with cornetts, and they were occasionally used for special effects in opera, a notable example being Monteverdi's *Orfeo* (1607).

Around 1740 the bell was widened in order to produce a stronger sound, but already the instrument was losing favour in many parts of Europe, and in England for a long time the only trombone players were to be found in the King's private band. In Germany and Austria, however, the instrument was played to a greater extent, being incorporated into notable dramatic scores, such as Gluck's *Orfeo* (1762), Mozart's *Magic Flute* (1791) and Haydn's *Creation* (1798). Georg Wagenseil (1715–77) wrote one of the earliest trombone concertos. With Beethoven's use of the alto, tenor and bass instruments in his *Fifth, Sixth* and *Ninth Symphonies*, the trombone gradually gained a foothold in the symphony orchestra, at first being used for harmonic rather than melodic purposes. Later the alto instrument was replaced by a second tenor playing in its high register. A contrabass was called for by Wagner in *The Ring*, and is still needed occasionally for other works. Although valves had been applied to certain trombones by 1830, these instruments came to be used mainly in military bands, as they are easier to play while marching. Most orchestral performers, however, still prefer to use the traditional instrument.

136. (Left) Bass trombone and shawm, with cornett and tenor violin above. On the left are a recorder, harp and lute. Detail from *The Glory of the Angels* by Ludovico Caracci (1555–1619). *Bologna, Church of San Palo.*

— CHAPTER VII —

Free Reed Instruments

A free reed is a small tongue of metal, one end being attached to a frame, while the other vibrates freely through pressure or suction of air. The pitch depends on its length and thickness. The earliest known instrument to which this principle was applied was the Chinese *sheng* (Japanese *sho*) which is still played in the Far East after at least 3000 years. Its first reeds are thought to have been made of bamboo.

Such reeds did not become properly established in Europe until the late eighteenth century (those of the earlier regal were somewhat similar in shape, but fixed to beat against their frame, so were not 'free'), apparently after the Jesuit missionary Père Joseph Amiot had sent a *sheng* from China to Paris in 1777. Soon afterwards, free reeds were the subject of much experimentation. The Abbé Georg Joseph Vogler, who was eager for novelty, built them, not only into church organs, but also in his transportable 'orchestrion' with which he toured Europe from 1789 onwards.

It was not long before organs were being built with free reeds and no pipes, in order to save space. The first of these was the **Orgue expressif** devised by Gabriel-Joseph Grenié of Paris in 1810. It was followed in 1818 by the **Physharmonica** of Anton Häckl of Vienna, an instrument which was connected to a piano and sounded with it. (This name was also applied to related instruments by other makers.) An English version was the **Seraphine**, made by John Green of London in 1834. In all these instruments the bellows were worked by pedals, as they were also in the **Harmonium** (originally with one pedal) by Alexandre-François Debain of Paris in 1840. This was distinguished by having four registers, and later there were added devices for graduating the dynamics. Its reeds vibrated through pressure of air as opposed to suction, which was used in the otherwise similar **American organ**, which has been made in the United States since 1856. Since that time the number of registers has increased, and nowadays small harmoniums are made with the air provided by an electric blower. Although used in its own right in domestic circles, the harmonium is perhaps most useful when deputizing for other instruments, whether it be for a church organ or in an amateur orchestra.

137. Harmonium by Mason & Hamlin, Boston, 1878. *Portsmouth, City Museum and Art Gallery.*

138. Harmonica with carved ivory covers. Viennese, 1880–85. *Trossingen, Matth. Hohner AG.*

The author will never forget playing, in 1948, in a thrilling school performance of Beethoven's *Egmont* Overture; nearly all the wind parts were supplied by a small organ and two harmoniums, as few of the right instruments were readily available in the post-war period.

European **mouth organs** date back to 1821, when Friedrich Buschmann started to experiment in Berlin. His **Aura**, at first having 15 and later 20 notes (every adjacent pair being produced by pressure and suction alternatively through one mouth-hole), was the ancestor of today's **Harmonica**. Meanwhile in 1829 Charles Wheatstone of London made a **Symphonium**, consisting of a box with one mouth-hole, and finger buttons to control the flow of air to the reeds. Buschmann's Aura, by now called **Mundharmonica** (**mouth harmonica**) found its way to the village of Trossingen between the Black Forest and the Alps, where, since 1857, it has been made by the firm founded by Matthias Hohner. Today the simplest harmonicas are still diatonic, but most now have a slider stop which raises the pitch by a semitone. Other models include those which provide chordal accompaniment to

139. Accordion (Gola 454 model) by Hohner.

the diatonic instruments, and compound harmonicas in as many as six keys. The virtuosity of Larry Adler and others has raised the harmonica to the dignity of a concert soloist and has inspired the writing of concertos for it by such eminent composers as Vaughan Williams. A more recent development by Hohner is the **Melodica**, which has one mouthpiece leading to a more-or-less rectangular case in which the reeds are controlled either by buttons or by a piano-type keyboard. It is much used in schools.

The **accordion** dates back to the diatonic **Handaoline** made by Buschmann in 1822, and followed seven years later by the **Akkordion** of Cyril Damian of Vienna. Its hand-blown bellows were terminated at each end by a box containing reeds controlled by finger buttons. The right hand played a diatonic melody, and the left a simple chordal accompaniment. Since *c.*1855 the Accordion has been chromatic. Mariano Dallape of Stradella, Italy, substituted piano keys for the right-hand buttons on certain models, giving rise to the name **piano accordion.** Other developments have included the addition of stops and couplers and a great

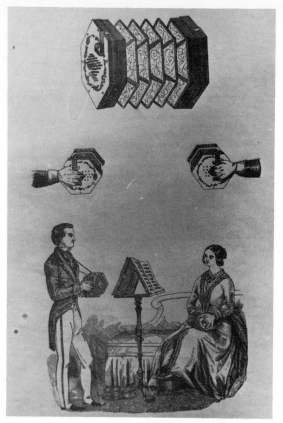

140.   Concertinas, as seen in the frontispiece to *Chidley's Instructions for the Concertina*, London, *c*.1854. *London, Royal College of Music.*

number of bass chords, while some of the most expensive (but not necessarily the best) have electronic effects such as vibrato and the sounds of orchestral instruments.

The **Concertina** was the result of Charles Wheatstone's applying the bellows of the accordion to his own Symphonium, a process which was completed in 1844. Between the buttons of both hands a chromatic scale could be played, but it was not until the later 'duet system' that each hand alone was completely chromatic. During the nineteenth century the concertina attracted virtuosi such as the London-based Giulio Regondi who was already an expert on the **Mélophone** (a guitar-shaped instrument with free reeds, bellows and a keyboard, invented by the Parisian clockmaker Leclerc). His two concertos are among numerous compositions which include, besides chamber music in which the concertina is played with more usual instruments, an *Adagio for Eight Concertinas in E* by Edouard Silas, one-time professor of harmony at the Guildhall School of Music, London.

— CHAPTER VIII —
Percussion Instruments

Percussion instruments, which by their nature involve a striking or clashing action, can be divided into three main categories: *idiophones*, which when played give out their own natural sound, *membranophones*, which depend for their pitch on a membrane stretched over a resonator, and *chordophones*, involving struck strings. There will also be treated here some shaken, plucked and rubbed idiophones which by their musical context fit best into this chapter. Membranophones will be considered first, as they include the percussion instruments of greatest historical importance, namely drums.

The antiquity of **drums** cannot be doubted, various different shapes and sizes (some of them very large indeed) appearing in Mesopotamian art dating from the third millennium BC. In Europe they have since been of three main types: cylindrical drums in which both ends of the cylinder are normally covered with a membrane; frame drums in which the diameter of the head is longer than the length of the side, and one or both ends are covered; and bowl-shaped drums, covered only on top.

The last-mentioned have in the long run been the most important in European art music under the general name *kettledrums*. Although the Babylonians had very large instruments of kettledrum shape *c.*1100 BC, and the Greeks had shallow bowl-shaped drums in the 6th century AD, the continuous European history of the orchestral timpani only goes back to the thirteenth century AD, when the Arabic *naqqāra* were adopted by the Crusaders, and in England, from *c.*1300, given the name **nakers**. Joinville, in his *Life of St Louis* (completed in 1309), tells us that at the battle of Mansourah on 8 February 1250, 'King Louis came up at the head of his battalions, with a great noise of shouting, trumpets and nakers' ('. . . a grand noyse et a grand bruit de trompes et de nacaires'). The nakers were small kettledrums played in pairs, of which each one was tuned to a different note. In England they were usually played at the performer's waist, while on the Continent they were also placed on the back of a servant or an animal, while the drummer walked behind wielding the sticks.

In the fifteenth century larger paired drums also came from the East, being used particularly by cavalry regiments, and suspended one on each side of a horse. Praetorius gave evidence of their having tuning screws in the seventeenth century, at which period the known pitch was generally *d* or *c* for the tonic and *A* or *G*

141. Drums and pipes played at Pharaoh's feast in a 6th-century Greek illustration from *The Book of Genesis,* chapter 40. Vienna, Österreichische Nationalbibliothek, Cod. theol. graec.31, f.34.

respectively for the dominant, to suit the pitch of the trumpets. By 1700 these cavalry drums were often used with trumpets in orchestral works of a ceremonial nature, and were called **timpani**. As their orchestral use increased, so they were adapted for it. For instance, greater scope was allowed to the harmony by tuning them to a fifth instead of a fourth (i.e. to the tonic with the dominant *above*) as was sometimes done from the time of Bach onwards. Gradually other intervals were specified within the limits of the two drums, reaching the extreme of an octave in Beethoven's *Eighth* and *Ninth Symphonies.* Berlioz experimented to a considerable degree, announcing in his *Treatise on Instrumentation* that

> to obtain a certain number of chords in three, four, and five parts, more or less doubled, and furthermore to achieve the striking effect of very close rolls, I have employed in my grand Requiem Mass eight pairs of differently-tuned kettledrums and ten drummers.

Such numbers were unusual, however; since the time of Weber three drums have often been used, while four, five or more are exceptional. Other investigations by Berlioz included the use of drumsticks with ends of wood, wood covered by leather, and sponge.

Until the time of Beethoven and Weber the tuning depended on the adjusting of square-headed screws with a separate tuning key. This lengthy process then gave way to built-in T-shaped screws which could be manipulated more easily and enabled the pitch to be changed, if necessary, between or even within movements, provided the performer had sufficient rest from playing. Experiments to simplify

142. Nakers, played in a margin of *The Romance of Alexander*, illustrated by Jehan de Grise in Flanders, 1338–44. *Oxford, Bodleian Library, MS. Bodl. 264, f.149v.*

143. (Right) Timpani, from the *Musikalisches Theatrum* of Johann Christoph Weigel, Nuremberg, before 1740, Plate 15.

the tuning still further included a device produced by Gerhard Cramer of Munich in 1812; it consisted of a central screw which could turn all the others at once.

From 1843 onwards different systems have involved the use of a pedal, which not only simplifies tuning but makes possible such musical devices as *glissandi*. Although such machine drums are regularly used in orchestras today, hand-tuned timpani are still frequently played.

In Greek and Roman times the frame drum was called **tympanon** or **tympanum** respectively, and its chief use seems to have been in rites honouring Cybele and Dionysus. Whatever may have happened to them in the Dark Ages, such drums were known again in Romanesque Europe, exemplified by a carving on an eleventh-century capital in the cloister of the abbey of Moissac. Gradually more shapes emerged, some of them being in primitive forms. A barrel, for instance, forms the resonator of the cylindrical drum in the much-reproduced picture of 'profane' instruments in the twelfth-century MS B.18, f.1, at St John's College, Cambridge (which, incidentally, was long thought to be English, but is now known to come from Rheims). Its shape, however, may have been inspired by the long cylindrical drum which had already come from the East to Byzantium where by that time it was highly developed. From the thirteenth century, European drums included not only the single-headed frame drum known as the **tambour**, but also the double-headed one and the longer cylindrical drum which were both covered by the name **tabor**. These were often played with the three-holed pipe (see page 113). The tabor often had a snare, and a fourteenth-century carved stall front in Lincoln Cathedral shows it to have been tunable by that time in England (a practice which had long been known in the East). Each pair of adjacent cords passing diagonally from one side to the other was threaded through a small piece

of leather which could be pushed up or down, thus tightening or loosening the tension and so raising or lowering the pitch. The mediaeval instrument was sometimes hit with two sticks (straight or shaped at the end), but more often with one, even when no pipe was involved. A fifteenth-century Dutch manuscript in the Bodleian Library (MS Douce 248, f.13) shows the stick of a pipe-and-tabor combination decorated with small bells.

It is worth noting that the word *symphony*, while generally applied to an instrument of the hurdy-gurdy family, was sometimes used also for the mediaeval tabor. John of Trevisa's translation of *De Proprietatibus Rerum* (see page 22) leaves no doubt over the matter:

> The Symphonye is an Instrument of Musyk: and is made of an holowe tree closyd in lether in eyther syde And Mynstralles betyth it wyth styckes And by accorde of hyghe and lowe therof comyth full swete notes.

From this time the tabor grew larger and was often held down at the side of the performer, hence the name **side drum**. (While the word *drum* is generic today, it only came into the English language in the sixteenth century.) Frequently played with the fife, it became an important ingredient of military bands, and has played an increasing part in the orchestra since the time of Handel. Other forms of side

144. (Left) Tympanum, played with tibia (left) and cymbals (right) for dancers on a vase painted by Polignotus, *c.*440–430 BC. *Ferrara, Museo di Spina.*

145. (Right) Tabor, formerly played by a devil on a 16th-century misericord. Like so many church carvings in England, this was damaged during the Reformation, and the devil's arm and drumstick broken off. *London, Westminster Abbey, Chapel of Henry VII.*

146. Bass drum, side drum, single and paired cymbals, with pedal timpani in the foreground. *London, Royal College of Music.*

147. Tambourine, played by one of the twelve musical angels on the 14th-century Minstrels' Gallery at *Exeter Cathedral*.

148. Cymbals, in one of their many mediaeval shapes, from the 15th-century stained glass (restored) of *Evreux Cathedral*.

drum include the snareless **tenor drum**, dating from the 1830s and played with soft beaters, and the large **bass drum** (at first called **long drum**) which appeared in the orchestra in the eighteenth century to play in 'Turkish' style music. This also had no snare. It was enlarged soon after 1800, and now has a prominent place in the orchestra. set in a frame in such a way that it can be turned to any suitable position. In 1857 Messrs Distin of London patented their **Monster Bass Drum** which, having a diameter of eight feet, was used only for very special occasions, such as the Handel Festival in 1865. Before its appearance in the first Hoffnung Concert in 1956, a door of London's Royal Festival Hall had to be removed to let it in.

The tympanon or tympanum of Greece and Rome sometimes had jingles on its frame, and in this form was later described as **tambourine** or **timbrel**. Mediaeval representations only became widespread shortly before 1300, often having a snare and sometimes small bells instead of jingles. Many Italian paintings of the Renaissance show it with both together, and occasionally with no skin. It was normally hit by the hand or fingers. The Baroque period was one of the times when the tambourine was unfashionable in art music (as it had been in fifteenth-century France and Flanders), but it reappeared among the 'Turkish' instruments which became popular in the late eighteenth century, and has been a fairly regular member of the orchestral percussion department ever since.

Among the oldest idiophones in art music are the round **cymbals**, of which several bronze pairs survive from Antiquity, ranging in size from small finger-cymbals to others of sixteen inches in diameter, as seen in the City Museum at Pompeii. Cymbals of classical Greece and Rome, and also those of mediaeval

149. Triangle player balancing two
candles on a rod held in his mouth. Detail
from an early 14th-century Flemish Book
of Hours. *Cambridge, Trinity College,
MS. B.11.22, f.148.*

Europe in general, were either deep in shape or almost flat with a slight central
dome, like those of today. Traditionally associated with Turkey, they have, since
1623, been made predominantly by the Armenian family of Zildjian, at first in
Constantinople and now in America. While the earlier method of playing seems
to have involved clashing them directly together (as shown so often in the visual
arts), more recent techniques have included brushing them against each other,
hitting them with drumsticks (hard or soft) and, in Bartók's *Sonata for Two
Pianos and Percussion* (1937), tapping them very quietly with the blade of a
penknife. A large orchestral cymbal is now often suspended on a pole, and sometimes connected to a bass drum so that one performer can easily play on both.
Berlioz said of the cymbals:

> Combined with the high tones of the piccolo and with the strokes of the
> kettledrum, it is particularly suited to scenes of unbridled wildness or to the
> extreme frenzy of a bacchanalian orgy.

Related to the single cymbal is the **gong**, a metal disc with its rim bent inwards.
Although it is particularly connected with the Far East, a Roman example dating
from the 1st or 2nd century AD was excavated in Wiltshire and can now be seen
in the Devizes Museum. The use of the gong in European orchestras seems to date
from the eighteenth century, when Gossec called for it in his *Funeral Music for
Mirabeau* (1791). It is also known by the name of **tam-tam**.

Very small cymbals described as **crotales** were often fixed to a forked piece of flexible wood or metal to form **clappers**, and as such were portrayed in the arts from ancient Egypt to the early Middle Ages. Other clappers of equal antiquity were made only of wood. In the Romanesque period paired wooden blocks were associated particularly with Spain, but from *c*.1300 they spread over most of Europe, similar instruments sometimes being made of bone. It is only from the fifteenth century that clear pictures emerge of the smaller and rounder **castanets** which are still connected so much with Spanish music. Single and paired wooden blocks (the latter called **Chinese** or **temple blocks**) are often beaten with sticks in contemporary music.

The **triangle** has a comparatively short history. Although seen in the thirteenth-century stained glass of León Cathedral in its simplest form, that of a plain metal triangle hit with a beater, it does not appear frequently in the arts until after 1300. The earliest English picture which has yet come to light is in the mid fourteenth-century glass of the Lady Chapel at Ely Cathedral, where the instrument has small bells attached to the lower bar. More often there were metal rings suspended from the bar, a custom which continued for several hundred years. The triangle is another of the instruments which, adopted mainly from the Turkish Janissary bands, entered orchestral scores in the eighteenth century, and has been increasingly used ever since.

Shaken idiophones are so numerous that only a few can be mentioned here. Among the most simple is the **rattle** consisting of a gourd filled with seeds or pebbles, now the **maraca** of American Indians. Shown with other instruments in the arts of mediaeval Spain, it has now moved into the orchestral world by inclusion in such works as Messiaen's *Turangalíla Symphony*.

The Egyptian **sistrum**, which was used by the Romans in the cult of Isis, consisted of a metal frame across which were stretched loose bars sometimes holding jingles, the whole instrument being shaken from a handle below. At the temple of Amon-Mut-Khons, a relief in the great colonnade of King Amenhotep III (1402–1364 BC) shows acrobats or dancers performing to the sounds of four sistra. The sistrum spread to Greece and Rome, and an example from Pompeii is preserved at the Museo Nazionale, Naples. Its nearest mediaeval equivalent was the triangle with jingles or bells. Small bells, however, were often worn by mediaeval people on their clothes, as can be seen in many pictures such as that of the Shaftesbury Psalter (plate 178), while the will of Alice Barbour of Salisbury, dated 1407, says 'I bequeath to my son John . . . my fifth ring of gold and a green girdle appareled with bells'.

The **Turkish Crescent** or **Jingling Johnnie** (French **chapeau chinois**) is known to have existed in the sixteenth century, and became one of the most spectacular instruments surrounding the Turkish sultan. It consisted basically of a pole on which were fixed various metal ornaments, one of them resembling a Chinese hat, and above it a Turkish crescent. The sounds were produced by numerous small bells or other jingling devices when the instrument was shaken. European regiments made great efforts to acquire Jingling Johnnies. One of those at the Royal Military School of Music, Kneller Hall, London (plate 151), was captured from

150. Sistrum, played by the Egyptian goddess Isis in a Roman statue. *Rome, Museo Capitolino.*

151. Jingling Johnny of unknown origin. In 1812 it was captured by the 88th Connaught Rangers from the French, who in turn had taken it from the Moors. *London, Royal Military School of Music, Kneller Hall.*

the Moors by the French, who themselves lost it in 1812 to the 88th Connaught Rangers. Berlioz recommended four of them for his gigantic orchestra which never materialized (see page 220).

Idiophones can be tuned by being made in different sizes. Bells, for instance, which each give out one basic note, become part of a melodic instrument when several are arranged together in a prepared sequence. Such were the **chimebells (cymbala)** which lasted from the eleventh century, if not earlier, to the early sixteenth. Arranged in varying numbers on a rod or frame, they were hit with two hammers, generally hard but sometimes soft. Several manuscripts of the Romanesque period give the tuning as diatonic but with an added B♭. The keyboard **carillon** which appeared in the Netherlands after 1500 consisted of church bells in a tower being controlled from a keyboard, of which each note was played by a whole hand; many carillons also had pedals. This strenuous occupation was described in some detail by Burney when he visited Amsterdam in 1772:

At noon I attended M. Pothoff to the tower of the *Stad-huys*, or town-house, of which he is *carilloneur*; it is a drudgery unworthy of such a genius . . . he executed with his two hands passages that would be very difficult to play with the ten fingers; shakes, beats, swift divisions, triplets, and even *arpeggios* he has contrived to vanquish. . . . I never heard a greater variety of passages, in so short a time; he produced effects by the *pianos* and *fortes*, and the *crescendo* in

152. Chimebells played by David in the initial E(xultate Deo) while his minstrels play trumpet and harp. From the English Ormesby Psalter of the early 14th century. *Oxford, Bodleian Library, MS. Douce 366, f.109.*

153. (Left) Carillon at the Cathedral of Notre Dame, Antwerp. Marin Mersenne, *Harmonicorum Libri*, Paris, 1636, p. 160. *London, Royal College of Music.*

154. (Right) Tuned percussion instruments in an informal setting. Left, from back to front: marimba, vibraphone, glockenspiel; Centre, from back to front: tubular bells, tubophone; Right, cowbells, gongs. *Percussion Services Ltd., 17–23 Vale Royal, London N.7.*

the shake, both as to loudness and velocity, which I did not think possible upon an instrument that seemed to require little other merit than force in the performer.

In contrast to this technique is that of playing **handbells**, where each person can ring no more than four bells and the skill lies in the co-ordination between the different performers.

Under the name **glockenspiel**, bell-like sounds are produced by striking strips or tubes of metal or glass, either with beaters or by means of a keyboard. The first method is seen in Van de Venne's *Fête donnée en l'honneur de la Trève* of 1609 (now in the Louvre). Both Handel in *Saul* (1739) and Mozart in *The Magic Flute* (1791) wrote for instruments which gave the effect of bells by means of a keyboard, but it is not known whether they had actual bells or bars. Alternatives today are the **tubophone** in which horizontal tubes are struck, and **tubular bells** in which they are suspended vertically from a frame. The latter are often used as a substitute for real 'church' bells which appear in certain scores, mainly operatic. In 1886 Auguste Mustel invented the **celesta**, another keyboard form of glockenspiel, in which the metal bars are hit by soft hammers and there is a sustaining pedal. One of its earliest parts was in Tschaikowsky's 'Dance of the Sugar-plum Fairy' in the *Nutcracker Suite* (1892). The **lyra-glockenspiel** consists of a portable lyre shaped frame into which are fitted the bars or other tuned shapes. It has been much used in Continental military bands since the nineteenth century, and also appears in such grand processions as that of the Munich Beer Festival. Other tuned bells include sets of **sleigh bells** at different pitches, used strikingly by Mozart in his *Sleigh Ride* dance, K.605.

Related to the glockenspiel is the **xylophone**, which is of primitive origins and can still be found as a folk instrument in many parts of the world. It consists of tuned blocks of wood (arranged nowadays like a keyboard) hit with sticks or hammers, and has been known in Europe at least since the sixteenth century when Hans Holbein the Younger showed it being played by a skeleton in his series of woodcuts *The Dance of Death* (1523). Nevertheless it was apparently not written into scores until 1874, when Saint-Saens used it in his *Danse Macabre*. Before that time not even Berlioz had specified it, in spite of the performances around Europe by the Russian Jew Gusikow, who had so much impressed Mendelssohn. Today the orchestral xylophone is arranged to resemble a piano keyboard, with a separate resonator below each note, and a range of about four octaves from *c'*. An octave lower is the **marimba**, another form of xylophone based on folk instruments, and also having resonators. A further development is the **vibraphone**, devised by Hermann Winterhoff of the Leedy Drum Co. in America, *c.*1920. With bars of a light metal alloy, it is distinguished by a clockwork or electric mechanism which activates a fan giving a vibrato effect to the sound; it also has dampers.

From the late Middle Ages there are pictures of **musical glasses**, built in different sizes and sometimes tuned by water filled to different levels. At first they were struck (as shown in the stained glass made in 1447 by John Prudde for the Beauchamp Chapel in St Mary's Church, Warwick), but later there was developed a technique of rubbing the edge of each with a dampened finger. In London in 1746 Gluck played a concerto he had written for 26 drinking glasses and orchestra. In 1762 Benjamin Franklin caused the glasses to revolve by means of a treadle, calling his instrument the **Glass Harmonica**, but although works were written for it by Mozart, Beethoven and others, it had an adverse effect on the nerves of the performers and was not widely adopted.

Mention has already been made of instruments used for special effects, such as sleigh bells. Others include the **anvil**, used as far back as the time of Praetorius, and prominent in Wagner's *Rheingold*, when 18 were called for. When real anvils are not available, other metal contraptions can provide a substitute sound. The **wind machine** is a revolving barrel-shaped friction instrument, the sound getting higher or lower according to the speed at which it turns. Other effects include a huge strip of metal which when shaken gives the effect of **thunder**, hinged wood blocks which when clapped together sound like a **whip**, and a machine to create the sound of **breaking glass**.

An idiophone which fits into a category all of its own is the **Jew's harp**. Neither Jewish nor a harp, it is a metal frame placed against the mouth of the player who flicks its metal tongue with his finger, and, by altering the position of his mouth, causes the sounding of the harmonic series. Several examples have been dug up in cemeteries from Roman times onwards. For a long time it was thought that one of the angels on the Minstrels' Gallery at Exeter Cathedral was playing a Jew's harp. In 1976, however, when the paint was being renovated by Anna Hulbert, it was found that the instrument in question had actually been a trumpet which later got broken off just beyond the mouthpiece. A good Renaissance illustration of a Jew's harp being played can be seen in *The Triumphs of Maximilian*, where the performer is one of the fools of the emperor's court.

155. Glass harmonica made in Germany, c.1780. *London, Horniman Museum.*

156. Miscellaneous instruments. Back, from left: (on stand) wood block, 4 Chinese temple blocks, triangle; (centre) wind machine; (right) paired orchestral cymbals. Front: (left) anvil; on table: (back) sleigh bells; (front, left to right) castanets, finger cymbals, 'bones', ratchet, maracas. *Percussion Services Ltd., 17–23 Vale Royal, London N.7.*

Most chordophones are plucked or bowed, or played by means of a keyboard with a plucking, striking or rubbing mechanism. Relatively few are struck directly by a beater held by the performer. The most simple of these is a **string drum** seen in Continental art from the fourteenth century onwards, but rarely, if ever, in English sources. Described by Jean Charlier de Gerson (1363–1429) in his *Tractatus de Canticis* (1423) as 'chorus', its shape was based on that of the monochord, with two or more strings generally tuned to the tonic and dominant. These were struck by a wooden stick to provide a rhythmical drone accompaniment to other instruments, most often the three-holed pipe, and in this combination it can still be found in southern France under the names *tambourin de Béarn* or *tambourin Basque*. A similar folk instrument to have survived in Hungary is the *gardon*, which is made in a shape resembling that of a cello.

More important historically is the **dulcimer**, which started life as a psaltery hit with beaters, instead of being plucked. This method is shown on the ivory cover of the Melissenda Psalter (British Library MS Eg. 1139), made of Byzantine craftsmanship in Jerusalem between 1131–43, but its appearances in European sources are rare until after 1400. (One earlier example can be seen in a late thirteenth-century sculpture in the west doorway at St Martin's Church, Colmar.) At this time the strings were single or double, and parallel to each other in the same plane. Some instruments had a bridge dividing the strings so that they each gave a different note on either side of it. Already before the time of Praetorius the

157.   Pipe and string drum similar to the tambourin de Béarn. Detail from the Milanese Book of Hours made for the Sforza family, *c*.1494. *London, British Library, MS. Add.34294, f.36v.*

courses had become triple (as they had in the Persian *santūr* about 300 years earlier), and another bridge had appeared. When this was at the right-hand end of the instrument its strings had the longest possible sounding length and gave the lowest notes. The strings passed alternately over one bridge and under another, sloping in such a way that the performer had greater freedom for striking than before. Gradually more bridges (or sets of small ones) were used to suit individual tuning requirements, the range of pitch was extended, and the instrument became fully chromatic. One of the greatest innovators was the German virtuoso Pantaleon Hebenstreit (*c*.1667–1750), who enlarged the dulcimer to over nine feet in length, and gave it gut as well as metal strings. He toured Europe playing his own compositions on it, and caused Louis XIV to christen it the **Pantaleone**. Nevertheless, because of the great cost of its strings, this instrument was already in a dilapidated state when Burney saw it in Dresden in 1772, and the dulcimer never became a regular member of the musical scene in western Europe. (It was used mainly for special effects, such as when Samuel Pepys heard it being played 'among the Fidlers' for a puppet show in Covent Garden on 23 May 1662.) In Germanic countries, however, it has long been used for folk music under the name *Hackbrett* (chopping board), and in eastern Europe, particularly in Hungary where its specialist performers have tended to be Jews and gipsies, it is called *cimbalom*. The cimbalom was developed in the late nineteenth century by V.J. Schunda of Budapest, who gave it a range of four octaves, stood it on legs, and devised a

158. Dulcimer, in the form of a rectangular box. Detail from *The Virgin and Child* by Giovanni Boccati (*fl.* 1445–80). *Perugia, Pinacoteca Vannucci.*

damper mechanism operated by means of a pedal. In recent years this instrument has been used to a certain extent in the concert orchestra, one of its most notable compositions being the *Háry János* suite by Kodály.

159. Cimbalom by V.J. Schunda of Budapest, 1887, played by its owner, John Leach of London.

— CHAPTER IX —

Mechanical Instruments

Among Henry VIII's instruments in 1547 was 'An Instrumente that goethe with a whele without playinge uppon . . .'. Music without a performer was already known in Biblical times, when King David was fascinated by the sound of the north wind playing on the strings of his lyre, and in the tenth century St Dunstan was accused of sorcery because his harp played by itself. In later times instruments were made with the sole purpose of sounding in the wind, prominent among them being the gut-strung **Aeolian harp** and the **glass chimes.**

Wind power was often helped by water. Archimedes (c.287–212 BC) is said to have made a statue of an aulos player standing on a box, and when water was poured into its cistern, air was forced upwards through a tube in the player's body, emerging through his mouth into the reed of the aulos. Ktesibios, the inventor of the organ, made singing birds which apparently worked on the same principle, and in later times the Byzantine Emperor Theophilus (829–42) had a golden tree with birds singing in its branches, although it is not clear how they worked.

Church bells were first mechanized with the invention of clockwork in the Middle Ages. Then came the discovery that a barrel or cylinder, fitted with carefully placed pegs or pins, could set in motion the hammers to hit the bells. The number of bells was gradually increased, resulting by the sixteenth century in large automatic **carillons** in the towers of churches and town halls, particularly in the Low Countries, where they are still famous. In 1772 Burney described the carillon at the Royal Palace in Amsterdam as having a brass cylinder weighing 4474 pounds, and pinned with 7200 iron studs.

The next important instrument to be mechanized was the **organ,** in which the pins on the barrel led to the sounding of the pipes. The oldest surviving instrument of this type is the Salzburg *Hornwerk*, built in 1502 for the Hohensalzburg Castle, and still playing after various restorations. Originally it had one cylinder, but Leopold Mozart added others, including on them some of his own tunes. While the cylinder of this instrument is turned by a handle, other Renaissance mechanical organs were powered by water, such as that of the Villa d'Este at Tivoli, and the only surviving example, at Hellbrun near Salzburg. Detailed drawings of such organs were given by Athanasius Kircher in his *Musurgia Universalis*, published at Rome in 1650.

In contrast to single instruments were those in which several were played at

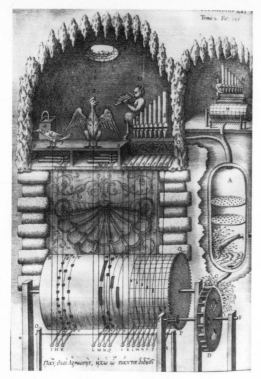

160. Design for a mechanical organ powered by water. Athanasius Kircher, *Musurgia Universalis*, Rome, 1650. *London, Royal College of Music.*

162. Barrel organ by Broderip & Wilkinson, London, *c.*1805. *London, Royal College of Music.*

once by one person. In the museum of musical wonders built by Michele Todini (*fl. c.*1650–*c.*1681) in Rome, the novelties included a combination of bagpipes and harpsichord (plate 161), besides a harpsichord and three spinets sounded from one keyboard. Handel is said to have played the organ through the keys of a harpsichord during performances of his oratorios. Related to such devices is the elaboration of manual organs by other instruments, a striking example being that of the Garrison Church in Berlin (made in 1724–25) as described by Burney:

> I found a large organ in this church, built by Joachim Wagner; it is remarkable for compass, having 50 keys in the manuals, and for its number of pipes, amounting to 3220; but still more so, for the ornaments and machinery of the case, which are in the old Teutonic taste and extremely curious.
>
> At each wing is a kettle drum, which is beat by an angel placed behind it, whose motion the organist regulates by a pedal; at the top of the pyramid, or middle column of pipes, there are two figures, representing Fame, spreading their wings, when the drums are beat, and raising them as high as the top of the

pyramid; each of these figures sounds a trumpet, and then takes its flight.

There are likewise two suns, which move to the sound of cymbals, and the wind obliges them to cross the clouds; during which time, two eagles take their flight, as naturally as if they were alive.

Among the completely mechanical instruments which appeared in the eighteenth century were small cylinder organs made for teaching birds to sing. The **Serinette** was for canaries, the **Perroquette** for parrots and the **Merline** for bullfinches and blackbirds, and the music recorded on their pins included works by Lully and François Couperin. **Flötenuhr** or **flute clocks** were clocks containing a cylinder and organ pipes, and giving a flute-like sound. A keen maker of these was Primitivus Němec, librarian and cellist to Prince Esterhazy, and composers who wrote pieces especially for them included C.P.E. Bach, Haydn, Mozart and Beethoven. A larger instrument, known in the specific sense as the **barrel organ**, emerged *c.*1700 and was used a great deal in churches, particularly in England. Diderot, in his 'Projet d'un nouvel orgue' (*Mémoires sur différents sujets de mathématiques*, The Hague, 1748), wished that they could be more widespread 'in order to eliminate indifferent organists'. They were not, however, restricted to the performance of hymns and psalms, their repertoire depending on the choice pinned onto the barrel. Charles Dickens, in his essay *Crossing the Channel*, wrote

And now that Hazebroucke slumbers certain kilometres ahead, recall the summer evening when your dusty feet strolling up from the station tended hap-hazard to a Fair there, where the oldest inhabitants were circling round and round a barrel-organ on hobby horses, with the greatest gravity . . .

The cylinder **musical box** was initiated by the Swiss watchmaker Antoine Favre in 1796, and enjoyed great popularity for over 100 years. Its most usual mechanism involves a pinned cylinder and a metal comb with tuned teeth, the sound being

161. Combined harpsichord and bagpipes, apparently created by Michele Todini in 17th-century Rome. *New York, Metropolitan Museum of Art.*

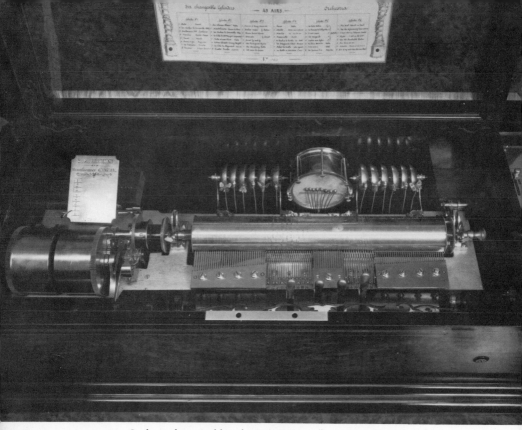

163. Orchestral musical box by B.A. Brémond & Co., Switzerland, *c.*1885–90. *Liverpool, City Museum.*

produced when a pin on the cylinder plucks a tooth of the comb. While this type of musical box still continues to be made (and its mechanism often enhances such objects as cuckoo clocks, cigarette boxes, Toby jugs and revolving fruit bowls) it was to some extent displaced by instruments of the **Symphonion** and **Polyphon** type, which appeared *c.*1890. Instead of a cylinder they had changeable metal discs stamped with projections which plucked at the comb. These, however, did not last long due to the early twentieth-century development of the **Gramophone** (originally **Phonograph**) which is with us today as a means of reproducing pre-recorded sound.

Meanwhile the change to more expressive and dramatic music in the late eighteenth century had brought into fashion large mechanical organs which imitated as many instruments as possible and were covered by the general name **orchestrion**. They are said to have been invented by J.G. Strasser, a clockmaker of St Petersburg, between 1789 and 1801, and were worked by the cylinder mechanism. One of the most celebrated was the **Panharmonicon** of Johann N. Mälzel of Vienna, which gave the sounds of strings, wind and percussion instruments. Having promised to make a hearing aid for Beethoven, Mälzel asked him to write a composition for this instrument, and the result was *Wellington's Victory or the Battle of Victoria* in 1813. The Panharmonicon was, however, soon to be

164. Instruments made by Friedrich Kaufmann and his family, on the occasion of their demonstration to Queen Victoria at Buckingham Palace in 1851. From left to right are the Harmonichord, Chordaulodian, Orchestrion, Automaton Trumpeter and Symphonion. *The Illustrated London News,* *5 July, 1851.*

outdone by the **Componium** (1821) of Dietrick Nicolaus Winkel of Amsterdam, who was enraged that Mälzel had poached his own idea of the *Metronome.* The Componium (which is now in the museum of the Brussels Conservatoire) was not only an orchestrion with nine stops and a triangle and drum, but it also contained a composing mechanism which made variations on whatever tune was fed into it, the ingenuity being such that to exhaust all the possibilities would take 138,000,000,000,000 years. A later development to the orchestrion family was the substitution, by Michael Welte of Freiburg in Breisgau (1807–80), of pneumatic action instead of the older pinned barrel method. Here the sounds were determined by the suction of air through a perforated paper roll which could easily be changed.

Among the most celebrated makers of mechanical instruments were the Kaufmann family of Dresden. In 1851 they demonstrated to Queen Victoria at Buckingham Palace their **Harmonichord** (similar to an upright grand piano but with the friction of a cylinder against strings of wire); their artificial **Trumpeter** whose instrument contained free reeds and could play more than one note at a time; their **Chordaulodian** which gave the sounds of flutes and strings; their **Symphonion** which imitated various instruments with piano accompaniment, and their **Orchestrion**. This last contained kettle and military drums, and triangle, besides effects for flutes, flageolets, clarinets, cornets, bugles, trumpets, bassoons, oboes, trombones, etc.

In contrast to these giants was the **organette**, a small reed organ with pneumatic mechanism, which was first popularized in America in the 1880s. Inevitably it led to larger instruments of the same type, one of the best being the **Orchestrelle** produced by the Aeolian Company from *c.*1898.

Like the organ, the piano also went through the pinned barrel stage, operated by a handle or by clockwork. A great change came in the late nineteenth century when pneumatic action was added to it in America (possibly by E.S. Votey), one of the most popular types being the **Pianola** of the Orchestrelle Company. At first this 'piano player' was a separate device, containing a perforated paper roll. It was pushed up to the keyboard of an ordinary piano, and when its air passed through the holes in the paper, 'fingers' played appropriate notes on the keyboard. The next stage was the 'player piano', where the pneumatic action and paper roll were built into the piano itself, and the hammers were hit by pressure of air from within. In these early designs there were devices by which a human being could control the interpretation, the general idea being well conveyed in an advertisement for the *Apollo Piano Player* – 'You supply the Expression and Soul. We supply the Technique.' The final stage came when the actual interpretations of great pianists were recorded on the rolls, as represented by the *Duo-Art Pianola* produced by the Aeolian Company from *c.*1898 onwards (see plate 202).

Because of the technical difficulties involved, the mechanization of bowed instruments has been comparatively rare, a notable example being the electro-magnetically-controlled **Virtuosa** produced in America in 1908, while pneumatic instruments include Stránský's **Violina** (1911) and the **Violiniste** of E. Aubry and G. Boreau (1920). Nevertheless, a remarkable demonstration was given to the Paris Conservatoire by M. Mareppe, in the form of an automaton violinist who played with a live orchestra and could obey the conductor. An account by the eye-witness M. Bruyère, made known in 1840, said that among other things

> he struck into a cadenza, in which the harmonics, double and single, arpeggios on the four strings, and saltos, for which Paganini was so celebrated, were introduced with the greatest effect; and after a close shake of eight bars, commenced the coda, a prestissimo movement, played in three parts throughout; this part of the performance was perfectly magical. I have heard the great Italian, and still greater Norwegian, Ole Bull; I have heard the best of music, but never heard such sounds as then saluted my ear. It began pianissimo, rising by a gradual crescendo to a pitch beyond belief, and then died away, leaving the audience absolutely enchanted. . . .

We have already seen how the mechanical instruments of the past were displaced by the gramophone. Now, however, they are rapidly becoming collectors' pieces, ranging from singing birds in snuff-boxes to gigantic orchestrions, and innocent-looking pieces of furniture such as the armchair belonging to King Frederick of Wurtemberg, which played when anyone sat on it. . . .

— CHAPTER X —

Instruments in the Twentieth Century

The twentieth century is a short time within the 5000 years covered by this book, but it deserves special attention on account of its greater variety of instruments and their treatment than any previous period in history. There follows here a brief summary of the main categories involved, but not, due to lack of space, a description of all the new instruments which have risen since 1900.

165. The string quartet, which is still flourishing after an existence of over 250 years. It is represented here by the Gabrieli Quartet: Kenneth Sillito and Brendan O'Reilly (violins), Ian Jewell (viola) and Keith Harvey (cello).

166. Traditional instruments in their mid 20th-century forms, played by members of the Melos Ensemble: Emanuel Hurwitz (violin), Neill Sanders (French horn), Gervase de Peyer (clarinet), William Waterhouse (bassoon), Cecil Aronowitz (viola), Adrian Beers (double bass) and Terence Weil (cello).

The instruments most played in art music today are still those of the average symphony orchestra, besides, of course, the piano and organ, all continuing their gradual process of evolution.

There is also a revival of interest in old instruments, pioneered in the early years of the century by Canon Francis Galpin and Arnold Dolmetsch. Many musicians now use Baroque, Renaissance and mediaeval-type instruments, but there is still insufficient knowledge as to which ones were used in specified periods and countries within the general term 'old'. Thirteenth-century music is only too often played on sixteenth- and even seventeenth-century instruments. One of the most recent revivals is that of nineteenth-century instruments, a welcome one which points out the great difference in sound between even that day and our own. Modern composers are now exploring the sounds of the past, not only for their historical value, but also because some of their very varied *timbres* blend well into modern idioms.

So much for ordinary instruments in their ordinary or revived conditions. One of the characteristics of modern music is their increasing use in extraordinary ways. The idea is not new. In the seventeenth century Carlo Farina called for the bow stick to be bounced on the violin strings (*col legno*) and for its hairs to play very close to the bridge (*sul ponticello*), which at that time may well have been regarded as outlandish. Today the *avant-garde* composers are exploring every possible way of making sounds come from an instrument. String players have to bow with the

167. Piano, played with a drumstick by Robert Sherlaw Johnson, a noted exponent of new techniques.

stick and hair together, to strike the strings with the wood of the bow between the bridge and the tailpiece, and to bow with excessive pressure 'so that the string creaks and jars'. Many instruments have to be 'scraped'. The woodwind and brass players are instructed to remove their reed or mouthpiece and blow through it separately, or to blow down the rest of the instrument without it, or just to rattle the keys without blowing at all. Harpists are told to 'play with the fingernails on the sounding-board', while pianists pluck the piano strings with their fingernails or play on them with drumsticks. The possibilities are unending. Often an instrument is 'prepared' by the presence of extraneous objects. While some of these methods jar one's nerves either by the sound they actually make or just by the very thought of potential damage to the instrument, others, when used by serious composers, can produce some very wonderful effects, and each piece of music must be judged on its merits. It is generally best to *see* these works being performed, as the visual aspect adds much to the overall effect.

There has been a great increase in the use of percussion instruments, those such as cowbells, African drums and Chinese wood blocks being already of some antiquity though not used for long in Western art music. Solo pieces, for example Stockhausen's *Zyklus* where one person plays on 13 different percussion instruments, require considerable versatility and virtuosity, and bear witness to the ever-growing number of expert percussionists.

The use of electricity in music has had far-reaching effects and is manifest in numerous ways. The least obvious is when it eases the performance of existing instruments, a notable example being the organ, which no longer needs a special person or persons to work the bellows. Somewhat related to this is the electrical actuation of the fans attached to the resonators of the vibraphone. In both these cases the performer's action is the same with or without electricity, which does not of itself affect the sound of the music. Professor Giles Brindley's **Logical Bassoon** and **Logical Contrabassoon** are instruments adapted, in the words of the inventor, 'to replace the mechanical linkage between the fingers and the note-holes by an electrical one', the aim being 'to preserve the timbre of the best notes, improve that of inferior notes, and make the player's task easier' (*GSJ* XXI, 1968, 152). While the timbre of the best notes is preserved, and the player still blows through a reed and controls the pitch by means of his fingers, the instrument's appearance has nevertheless changed from that of the traditional bassoon.

168.   The Logical Contrabassoon, played by its inventor, Giles Brindley.

Another category involves the use of microphones to enlarge the sound of a natural instrument. Here the sound is altered to a certain extent, whether in the process of making a recording, or in rendering the instrument more audible in a concert hall. This latter method has aroused much controversy when applied to such quiet instruments as the clavichord.

Further instruments, though retaining their original performing action, are adapted by built-in loudspeakers and amplifiers. These include the **Neo-Bechstein Piano** invented by Wilhelm Nernst in 1936. Retaining its keys, hammers, strings and sustaining pedal, it has 18 microphones which take the place of a soundboard, and an amplifier controlled by the left pedal. The **electric guitar** also bears some resemblance to its prototype by keeping its strings and fretted fingerboard, but the sound is quite different, and when magnified too much it becomes a public nuisance.

The largest category of electrical instruments is that in which frequencies are generated by electronic means, and magnified in different ways. Some of them, such as Lev Theremin's **Theremin** (*c*.1924), Friedrich Trautwein's **Trautonium** (1930) and Maurice Martenot's **ondes Martenot** (*c*.1928) are only melodic, sounding just one note at a time. One of the simplest shapes is that of the Theremin, which to the casual eye consists of a cabinet from which a metal rod projects

169.   The *ondes Martenot*, with its owner, John Morton, standing behind the keyboard. The *palme* is placed on top of the *principale*, with the *métallique* in front.

170.   Thaddeus Cahill's Telharmonium, the earliest electronic instrument. *The Illustrated London News, 23 February, 1907.*

171.   The Hammond *Monarch*, an electronic organ which, according to its 1976 advertisement, can 'create millions of sound variations to suit any musical mood or style'.

172. The E.M.S. (London) 'Synthi 100' studio synthesizer. *Electronic Music Studios.*

upwards. By moving his hand to or away from the rod, the player can raise or lower the pitch respectively. Too much *glissando* can be avoided by the use of control buttons. The ondes Martenot is nowadays in four distinct parts, one containing keyboard and controls, and the other three being diffusers of the sound. They are the *Principal*, which gives the most natural sound of the instrument, the *Métallique* which by means of a gong creates a metallic resonance, and the *Palme*, across which are stretched 24 strings. These give the effect of a viola or cello in *legato* passages, but of a harp when the playing is *glissando*. This effect is produced by pulling a ribbon adjacent to the keyboard.

The polyphonic instruments, those which can play more than one note at a time, include the oldest electronic instrument of all, the **Telharmonium** invented by Thaddeus Cahill in 1906 and erected in New York. Its gigantic machinery, controlled from a keyboard, was intended to produce music which could be played by telephone to those who wished to hear it. Unfortunately the plan had to be dropped, as the sounds interfered with the normal telephone wires. Later electronic organs appeared in the 1930s and have since been in great demand due to their relatively low cost and small size as compared to pipe organs, being used in churches, private houses, cinemas, schools and other institutions. One of the most frequently used is the **Hammond organ**, which has two manuals, a pedal-board, and the means of producing innumerable different types of sound.

All the instruments previously described have normally depended for their musical result on a single performer playing at a certain time. Since the Second World War a new process has been set in motion – that of mixing sounds to be used as required. Under the title *musique concrète* this can be done at the minimum by two tape recorders, but the subject has now been developed to such an extent that complete electronic studios are built to contain the necessary equipment. A prominent item is the **synthesizer**, a machine which can produce any sound for which it has been prepared. Certain models retain a visual connection with music by the presence of one or two keyboards, but others would not be recognized by the ordinary person as having anything to do with music. Nevertheless their potentialities for generating and synthesizing sounds are immense, and together with tape recorders, microphones, amplifiers, oscillators and other gadgets of the electronic studio, they provide stimulus to many composers, who often use their sounds together with those of 'live' instruments. Their overall value can only be judged at a later date in the light of history.

— CHAPTER XI —
The Development of Instrumentation

It is only within the last three centuries that composers have, with anything approaching regularity, specified the exact instruments for a given piece of music. Before that time instruments played a considerable part in the functions of daily life, whether as signals, as toys, for the private enjoyment of the players, or for the enrichment of special events, both sacred and secular; the choice of instruments, however, depended on what was available and suitable for the occasion.

From verbal descriptions and from the visual arts, we see that in ancient Greece and Rome the kithara and lyra often accompanied the voice, while wind and percussion instruments were more associated with dancing and pagan rites. Lucretius tells us that at a feast in honour of Cybele

> the taut drums throb to the beat of the palms, the hollow cymbals clash around them, the trumpets sound their harsh threat, and the Phrygian rhythm of the *tibia* stirs the soul.
>
> (*De Rerum Natura*, ii, 618–20.)

Organs were sometimes used in honour of the gods (see page 94), but in the Roman Empire they were frequently played in the circus to enliven the fights of gladiators; here they were accompanied by the cornu and tuba, both instruments of war.

For the centuries following the collapse of the Roman Empire we know little about the development of instrumentation, although there is enough evidence to show that the voice was generally accompanied by a stringed instrument, and that horns were played on ceremonial occasions. By the Romanesque period, however, two very important developments had occurred. One was the acceptance of the organ by the Christian Church, and the other was the appearance and widespread use of the bow.

The Church's attitude to the use of instruments in the liturgy has fluctuated throughout the ages, largely due to changing musical conditions. Hence the slow adoption of the organ because of its earlier pagan associations. By the twelfth century, however, it was well established in the more important churches (see page 96), while those who could not afford it may have had an organistrum instead. According to Honorius of Autun, chimebells and larger bells were, like

173. A gladiatorial fight enlivened by a tuba, two cornui and a hydraulis. Detail of a Roman mosaic of the 1st century AD, from a villa at Dar Buk Ammera, near Zliten, Libya. *Tripoli Museum.*

174. Symphony, organ and chimebells, in a picture from the *Rutland Psalter*, f.97v., made in England *c.*1270. *Rutland, Belvoir Castle.*

the organ, used to praise God (*Commentarius in Ps. 80, 4*), but soon afterwards St Ailred of Rievaulx said that the sound of the organ pipes and bellows, and the chimebells 'caused the ordinary people to stand with wondering faces, trembling and amazed' (*Speculum Caritatis*). These were the instruments definitely accepted by the mediaeval Church, but others were occasionally allowed, as witnessed by two English scholars of the thirteenth century who spent time in Paris and heard the music of the school of Notre Dame. The theorist described by Edmond de Coussemaker as 'Anonymous IV', said in his *De Mensuris et Discantu* that the sounds of strings or pipes ('cordarum vel fistularum') could be used to double the voices at upper octaves in organum; while his 'fistulae' may well have been organ pipes, this cannot be said for the 'cordae'. Magister Lambertus (mistakenly known as 'Pseudo-Aristotle'), having mentioned in his *Tractatus de Musica* 'organa, vielle, cythara, cytole, psalterium et similia', added that they were now daring to creep into church. By 1500, trumpets, shawms, cornetts and sackbuts often enriched the liturgy for special events, either playing on their own or doubling the voices. Dufay's four-part *Gloria* 'ad modum tubae' is one of several pieces where textless parts are playable on trumpets, but as yet it was rare for such instrumentation to be specified. (The words 'ad modum' may also imply vocal imitation of the sound of trumpets.) Since the Reformation the multiplicity of religions has led to even greater diversity of instrumental practice than before, so for the rest of this chapter any reference to liturgical music will be within its purely musical context.

There are a good many mediaeval references to instruments being played in church on completely unliturgical occasions, such as when the Princess Eleanor, sister of Edward III, was travelling from London to Holland in 1332 to marry the Count of Guelders. She stopped at St Paul's Cathedral to leave an offering at the great *Crux Borealis* in the North Chapel, and her subsequent expense accounts reveal payments to several fiddlers ('diuersis vidulatoribus') who played there. Portable instruments were often used in processions, particularly outside the church when the organ could not be heard. When Duccio's celebrated painting, the *Maestà*, was taken into the Cathedral of Siena on 9 June 1311, it was accompanied by the sounds of trumpets, shawms and nakers, as befitted a great occasion.

Very little secular music has survived from before the twelfth century, and no

177. David playing a fiddle on his lap, surrounded by musicians with, from left to right: lute, portative (?) organ, panpipes, horn and psaltery; other instruments are out of the picture. Detail from a capital carved *c*.1100 at *Jaca (Spain) Cathedral.*

178. A typical Romanesque grouping of instruments, and one which sounds well in reconstructed performance. Musicians in the initial B(eatus vir) play a rebec, harp, and primitive drum. The drummer, who is dressed as an animal, has bells on his fingers and round his ankles. Detail from *The Shaftesbury Psalter*, illustrated in England *c*.1130–50. *London, British Library, MS. Lans; 383, f.15v.*

completely instrumental pieces are known from before the thirteenth. This was the time when most minstrels could not read or write words, let alone music, so most of what they played was passed on from one person to another, or improvised on the spur of the moment and never played again. This accounts for the lack of surviving early instrumental dance music, although certain songs, such as *Tuit cil qui sunt enamourat, viegnent dançar* (which may come from the court of Eleanor of Aquitaine), were intended for dancing and would often have involved instruments. A rare suggested specification in a Troubadour song occurs in Peire D'Alvernhe's satirical *Chantarai d'aquetz trobadors*, which ends with the lines 'This poem was made for bagpipe players ["enflabotz"] at Puivert, in sport and laughter'. Mediaeval methods of accompanying a monophonic song or dance included doubling the melody, playing in heterophony around it, droning below or above it (if the melody could take a drone), playing it at a set interval apart, or playing solo passages at the beginning and end, with an interlude between each verse. In the *Tristan* of Gottfried von Strassburg, for instance, we read that

> Tristan . . . drew his snatches and preludes, his haunting initial flourishes so sweetly from his harp and made them so melodious with lovely string music, that all came running up, one calling another.

The treatment, however, would vary according to circumstances. The earliest known instrumental dances, both monophonic and polyphonic, date from the thirteenth century, as also do some three-part textless motets in French sources. One of these is called *In seculum viellatoris*, suggesting that the player of a mediaeval viol or fiddle may have taken the tenor part, which is based on the melody for the words 'in seculum' from the Easter Gradual, *Hec dies*.

179. Fiddle and gittern played together for dancing in the initial D(eus), from an English Book of Hours, *c.*1250–75. *London, British Library, MS. Eg. 1151, f.*47.

The *Robertsbridge Fragment* (British Library MS Add. 28550), which dates from *c*.1325–50, contains the earliest known keyboard pieces, in the forms of dances and motet arrangements. Played by a positive organ, the dances would be accompanied to advantage by a tabor or tambourine, as shown in plage 181. Songs of this period, written by such composers as Machaut and Landini, contain textless lower parts which seem to indicate instrumental participation. Before 1400 the Monk of Salzburg referred somewhat ambiguously to the use of 'das Nachthorn', 'das Taghorn', 'das Kchuhorn' and 'die Trumpet' in connection with certain songs, but with another he made it clear that 'der Pumhart', a bumbarde, is to play the given accompaniment below the voice. The Monk's example, however, was not generally followed, and we have to search for descriptions of events to find out how music was actually performed. These can be tantalizing. The chroniclers of the celebrated Feast of the Pheasant, held at Lille by Philip the Good, Duke of Burgundy, on 17 February 1454, tell us of two trumpeters on horseback, of a model church containing singers, an organ and a bell, and of a pie (if the word 'pasté' really did mean a pie apart from its various other meanings) containing 28 musicians. From the church came singing and organ music and the bell, and from the pie the sounds of a German cornett, of a quartet of recorders, of a lady called Paquette singing with two fiddles and a lute, and of many other items, but we are not told of the music they played. For the two pieces which *are* mentioned by name, there is no reference to instruments.

By this time it was customary to play in groups of either loud (*haut*) or soft (*bas*) instruments. The former type would include trumpets, shawms and bagpipes, while among the latter would be harps, lutes, fiddles, portative organs, recorders,

180.   Minstrels at a feast, playing fiddle, symphony, harp and psaltery; the psaltery player appears to be giving a beat. Detail from a French *Bible Moralisée*, *c*.1250–75. London, British Library, MS. Harl.1527, f.36v.

181. Organ and tambourine played together in a Flemish Book of Hours, c.1300. (The organ has a drone pipe on the right.) *London, British Library, MS. Stowe 17, f.129.*

182. Singers accompanying themselves on a psaltery (*mezzo-canone*) and mandora, from a manuscript of *The Romance of King Meliadus* written for Louis II, titular King of Naples, between 1352–62. *London, British Library, MS. Add. 12228, f.222v.*

183. Trumpeters and shawm-players leading a procession, seen on a dish made at Caffagiolo in the late 15th century. *Rouen, Musée des Antiquités*.

184. Psaltery-harp and pipe played by David and one of his musicians in procession before the Ark of the Covenant. Woodcut by Heinrich Quentel of Cologne, in the *Biblia Germanica* printed at Nuremberg by Anton Koberger [17 February 1483]. The woodcuts were originally used in Quentel's Low German Bibles of 1478–80. *Durham, Dean and Chapter Library, Inc. 14a, f.145v*.

and other instruments suitable for indoor use. Many of them were extending their compass downwards (influenced by the descent of the human voice into the bass register in the mid-fifteenth century), with the result that by about 1500 there were certain families of different sizes aiming at some kind of standardization. When instruments of only one family were played together, the group was called a *whole consort*, while a *broken consort* was the continuation of the apparently older method of grouping together instruments of different tone qualities. Little of the consort music written during the sixteenth century had specified instrumentation, but we do know what instruments were used on certain occasions with the composers' consent. For instance, at the celebrations for the marriage of Cosimo I, Duke of Florence, to Eleonora of Toledo in 1539, Francesco Corteccia's music for the *intermedi* included:

a) the song *Vattene Almo riposo* sung by 'Dawn', accompanied by a harpsichord, organ, recorder, harp, voices of birds and a bass viol
b) the song *Vienten'almo riposo* sung by 'Night', accompanied by four trombones
c) the song *Bacco, Bacco, e u o e* sung by twenty bacchantes playing a drum, rebec, cornett, two crumhorns, a straight trumpet, a harp and a straight cornett, all of which were hidden among bones, branches and other disguises.

185. A consort of viols playing during the journey of Queen Louise of Lorraine from the Louvre to the Faubourg Saint-Marceau. From an anonymous drawing of 1584. *Paris, Bibliothèque Nationale.*

Towards the end of the century more compositions were written for suggested or specified instruments. The first volume of Giovanni Gabrieli's *Sacrae Symphoniae* (1597), which are mainly 'for voices or instruments', includes the completely instrumental *Sonata Pian'e Forte*. Its two 'choirs' consist of (a) one cornett and three trombones, and (b) one 'violino' (actually a viola) and three trombones. These instruments, besides an organ and 'fagotto' (curtall) appear more frequently, and often with independent parts, in the second volume, which was published posthumously in 1615. They are, incidentally, the instruments which, apart from the organ, appeared most often in the sacred music of the early Baroque period.

The chief part song of the Elizabethan age, the madrigal, was normally written out for voices. It could, however, also be doubled by instruments or played by them alone, as indicated by the frequent direction 'Apt for voyces or viols'. An important landmark in the history of chamber music came with Thomas Morley's *Consort Lessons*, published in 1599, for a flute, treble viol, bass viol, cittern,

186.   A broken consort consisting of trombone, two singers, organ, cornett, bass viol, violin and lute, from the German *Album* of Hieremias Buroner of Augsburg, 1592–9. *London, British Library, MS. Eg. 1554, f.2.*

187.   Singing choristers accompanied by cornett, two shawms, trombone and curtall, in *The Virgin of Montserrat* by Juan Ricci (1600–81). *Barcelona, Abbey of Montserrat.*

188. Angel musicians playing cornett, violin and organ, in a 17th-century wall-painting by Clemente Maioli. *Ferrara, Church of the Teatini.*

pandora and treble lute, without voices. It was from such broken consorts that the earliest opera and oratorio orchestras were formed. Emilio de Cavalieri's Introduction to the *Rappresentazione di Anima e di Corpo* (1600) suggests the suitability of such instruments as a double harp, harpsichord and chitarrone to be played behind the scenes, while at a given point a Spanish tambourine and Spanish guitar may be played on the stage by the actors. This work is also noteworthy for containing the earliest known printed figured bass part for the continuo, itself a recent development associated with that group of Florentine poets and musicians known as the *Camerata*. Monteverdi, in his opera *Orfeo* (1607), calls clearly for

189.   Three choirs of instrumentalists playing in the polychoral tradition derived from Venice. Praetorius, *Theatrum Instrumentorum* (1620), title page.

190. Singers accompanied by a rebec (or kit), sordun (?) and lute, with a cornett on the ground by the lute case. Detail from *A Festival in a Palace Garden* by Sebastian Vrancx (1573–1647). *Copenhagen, Royal Museum of Fine Arts.*

191.   An orchestra of (left) string and (right) wind players, with triangle.
Detail from the title page of Elias Nikolaus Ammerbach's *Ein New Kunstlich
Tabulaturbuch*, Nuremberg, 1575. *Munich, Bayerische Staatsbibliothek.*

192.   A string orchestra (perhaps containing some of 'The King's
Twenty-four Violins') playing in Westminster Hall during the banquet
celebrating James II's coronation on 23 April, 1685. Francis Sandford, *The
History of the Coronation of . . . James II*, London, 1687, after p. 118.
London, British Library.

Duoi Gravicembani
Duoi contrabassi de Viola
Dieci viole da brazzo
Un Arpa doppia
Duoi violini piccoli alla Francese
Duoi Chitaroni
Duoi Organi di legno
Tre bassi da gamba
Quattro Tromboni
Un Regale
Duoi Cornetti
Un flautino alla Vigesima Seconda
Un Clarino con tre trombe Sordine.

This is not just an assembly of any instruments which happened to be around. They were carefully selected to suit the dramatic effects required, a striking example being the use of a regal when Charon, the ferryman of the Underworld, challenges Orpheus at the shores of the river Styx. The aria *Possente Spirto* demonstrates the virtuosity of its players in the respective *obbligato* sections for two violins, two cornetts and the double harp.

Compositions using a basic string orchestra (of the violin rather than the viol family), although rare at this time, can be traced back at least to 1581, when *Circé, ou le Balet comique de la Royne* was performed at the French court to celebrate the marriage of the king's sister to the Duc de Joyeuse. This includes dances, written by Lambert de Beaulieu, which were performed by ten 'violons', actually different sizes of the violin family. Thus was set the tradition for the famous *Vingt-quatre Violons du Roi* established in 1626 by Louis XIII for his entertainment. The idea was adopted by Charles II on his accession to the English throne in 1660, and according to Pepys this new band played at the Coronation banquet on 23 April 1661. In the words of Roger North, it 'disbanded all the old English music at once', although Henry Purcell wrote viol fantasias as late as 1680. Meanwhile in France Lully had created in 1656 a select group, *Les Petits Violons*, which became renowned for its uniformity of bowing and general orchestral discipline. This was the basic orchestra (arranged for five string parts) used for his operas and ballets, with wind instruments added for special effects such as rustic or warlike scenes. In the ballet *Alcidiane* (1658), for instance, shepherds and shepherdesses danced to the sound of woodwind instruments, the music being directed by Lully who was dressed as a faun. The wind players came from the bands of the *Grande Ecurie* at Versailles, which by 1690 consisted of

Les trompettes
Les fifres et tambourins ou tambours
Les joueurs de violons, hautbois, saqueboutes et cornets
Les cromornes et trompettes marines
Les hautbois et musettes du Poitou.

193. Musicians at a feast, playing violin, spinet, violino piccolo, lute, tenor
violin and bass violin. Detail from *The Prodigal Son squanders his Inheritance*
by Stefan Kessler, 1662. *Innsbruck, Collection of Dr Hans Graf Trapp.*

After the oboe appeared as a result of refinements to the shawm by Jean Hotteterre and his colleagues, its first documented appearance in a specific part seems to have been in Robert Cambert's opera *Pomone* of 1671, (but see page 124). From that time it became a frequent member of the orchestra and of chamber music, generally supported on the continuo line by the newly developed bassoon.

A typical late seventeenth-century ceremonial orchestra is that for Purcell's Ode for St Cecilia's Day, *Hail Bright Cecilia*, which was first performed at a public concert in the Stationers' Hall, London, in 1692. The choruses are joined by strings, oboes, trumpets, kettle drums and continuo, while the solo voices are accompanied either by the continuo alone, or by the continuo with any of the above-mentioned instruments, or recorders, selected according to the mood of each movement.

While so much instrumental music was still connected with dancing, drama or singing, the seventeenth century saw great advances in purely instrumental forms and techniques. The old fantasias and canzonas, which so often reflected the Renaissance equality of voices, gave way to sonatas, in which there was more room for instrumental freedom and virtuosity above the supporting continuo. Although some of these works, and particularly trio-sonatas, still allowed for a choice of instrument, others were restricted by their idiom to one in particular. Such works are those violin sonatas by Biber and Corelli which by their double stopping preclude performance on a recorder, flute or oboe.

194.   A concerto played on harpsichord, strings, oboes and horns. *Zurich Musicalische Neu-Jahrs-Geschenke, 1744, Plate LX. London, British Library, Hirsch IV.1135, p. 473.*

It could be said that the coming-of-age of an instrument is achieved when a concerto is written for it. After Stradella and Corelli had paved the way with the *concerto grosso*, with its contrast of large and small instrumental groups, the solo concerto emerged in the works of Torelli and other composers working at the church of San Petronio, Bologna. The first solo concertos, which were written before 1700, were mainly for the trumpet and violin, two of the most experienced instruments in current use. Soon afterwards, Vivaldi was teaching in Venice at the *Ospedale della Pietà*, a girls' orphanage which produced very competent musicians. He not only provided them and others with new repertoire, but did great service to the instruments themselves, writing concertos for the violin, cello, mandoline, lute, recorder, flute, piccolo, bassoon, oboe and viola d'amore, besides numerous sonatas and *concerti grossi*. J.S. Bach used several concertos by Vivaldi as models for his own, transforming, for instance, a Vivaldi concerto for four violins into one for four harpsichords (*c.*1733).

Much of Bach's instrumental music was written at the court of Prince Leopold of Anhalt Cöthen, whose orchestra in 1717 included players of the violin, cello, viola da gamba, oboe, bassoon, trumpet and drums. It had no regular French horns, as these instruments were still comparatively new in orchestras. Gradually more pieces were written to include them, so freelance horn-players travelled in pairs playing where they could, and 'die beyden Waldhornisten' who visited Cöthen in 1722 may have taken part in a performance of Bach's *First Brandenburg*

195. A choral work, performed with strings and organ. *Zurich, Musicalische Neu-Jahrs-Geschenke, 1769, Plate LXXXV. London, British Library, Hirsch IV.1135, p. (279).*

Concerto. In this and other *concerti grossi* dedicated to the Margrave Christian Ludwig of Brandenburg in 1721, Bach used instruments which were, or were fast becoming, regular members of the orchestra, and in the *Fifth Brandenburg Concerto* he raised the role of the harpsichord to that of soloist. It was in his sacred music that Bach exploited the tone qualities of some of the more introspective instruments. In the *St John Passion*, for instance, the *arioso* 'Betrachte, meine Seel' is sung to the *obbligato* accompaniment of two viole d'amore and a lute. It was in sacred music, too, that the usual keyboard continuo instrument was the organ. Its role as a concerto soloist seems to have originated in Handel's oratorios, where concertos could be played on an organ, harpsichord or harp between the acts.

   Bach and Handel represented the culmination of an epoch, both in their writing and in their use of instruments. Yet already during their lifetime changes were taking place which radically altered the character of music. These changes are associated chiefly with Vienna, Mannheim and Paris, and are reflected particularly in early Germanic symphonies and Parisian operas. Counterpoint was to a great extent abandoned, together with the figured bass continuo part, although

196.   A military band consisting of horns, oboes and bassoons. Detail from: Zurich, Musicalische Neu-Jahrs-Geschenke, 1759, Plate LXXV. British Library, Hirsch IV, 1135, p. 593.

written-out or improvised keyboard parts remained in some orchestras until well after 1800. The bass viola da gamba, which had outlived most of the other viols by about a century, was not suited to the new music, and gave way to increasing pressure from the cello, which had already emerged from the larger bass violin before 1700. The transverse flute, which had long been used as an alternative to the recorder, finally took precedence in the mid-eighteenth century, partly due to the renowned musicianship of Frederick the Great, and also because of its greater suitability in the new 'expressive' music where the frequent *crescendi* and *diminuendi* would have wrought havoc with the intonation of a recorder. The timpani, the chief percussion instruments of the Baroque period, were now joined for special effects by the triangle, cymbals, tambourine and bass drum recently popularized by the Turkish Janissary bands.

The court of the Elector Carl Theodor at Mannheim contained an orchestra under Johann Stamitz and his successor Christian Cannabich, which was the most celebrated since that of Lully. In 1756 it had

10 first violins
10 second violins
 4 violas
 4 cellos
 4 double basses
 2 flutes
 2 oboes
 2 bassoons
 4 horns
 1 trumpet
 2 timpani

Clarinets were used as extras or instead of other instruments, and Stamitz himself wrote one of the earliest clarinet concertos. The discipline and attack of this orchestra, together with its cultivation of dynamic ranges, caused Dr Burney to describe it in 1772 as 'an army of generals'. He did, however, note

> an imperfection in this band, common to all others that I have ever yet heard . . . the want of truth in the wind instruments. I know that it is natural for those instruments to be out of tune, but some of that art and diligence which those great performers have manifested in vanquishing difficulties of other kinds, would surely be well employed in correcting this leaven, which so much sours and corrupts all harmony. This was rather too plainly the case tonight, with the bassoons and hautbois, which were rather too sharp at the beginning, and continued growing sharper to the end of the opera.

It was in outdoor music that wind instruments could sound their best, unhampered by the devastating effects of a hot orchestral pit. On the way to Mannheim Burney had passed through Darmstadt, where he

197.   The orchestra for Haydn's opera *L'Incontro improviso*, performed at Esterhaz in 1775. *Munich, Theatermuseum.*

was so fortunate, as to alight from my chaise just as the landgrave's guards were coming on parade. I never heard military music that pleased me more; the instruments were, four hautboys, four clarinets, six trumpets, three on each side the hautboys and clarinets, and these were flanked by two bassoons on each side; so that the line consisted of eighteen musicians; in the rear of these were cornets and clarions.

The whole had an admirable effect, it was extremely animating, and though trumpets and clarions are usually too shrill and piercing, when heard in a small place, yet here, the parade or square where they mounted guard is so spacious that the sound has room to expand in all directions, which prevents the ear from being hurt by too violent a shock.

Earlier in the year he had also been pleased with very varied bands at Ghent:

the one was an extra-band of professed musicians, consisting of two hautbois, two clarinets, two bassoons, and two French horns; the other were enlisted men and boys, belonging to the regiments; the number of these amounted to twenty. There were four trumpets, three fifes, two hautbois, two clarinets, two *tambours de basque* [tambourines], two French horns, one crotolo or cymbal, three side-drums, and one great kettle-drum. All these sonorous instruments, in the open air, have a very animated and pleasing effect.

Apart from military bands, the performers of outdoor music included serenading parties, itinerant musicians and students. Some of the latter were taught at music schools attached to Jesuit colleges, and were heard by Burney in the streets of Munich

> where they performed some full pieces very well: there were violins, hautboys, French horns, a violoncello, and bassoon. I was informed, that they were obliged frequently to perform thus in the streets, to convince the public, at whose expence they are maintained, of the proficiency they make in their musical studies.

Such outdoor music encouraged complete independence of parts, as a keyboard instrument was not always available to fill in the harmony. A harp, however, was sometimes used in street music.

The gradual rejection of the continuo was also evident in chamber music, where trio sonatas gave way to trios and quartets without an accompanying keyboard instrument. Alessandro Scarlatti (1660–1725) had written, during the last years of his life, *Sonate a quattro: Due Violini, Violetta e Violoncello – senza cembalo.* These could be performed by one or more players to each part, as could the early string quartets of Haydn, the first dating from before 1755. Of the wind instruments, oboes and flutes were already well experienced in chamber music, while bassoons had been used mainly as part of the continuo. Now the greater independence for these and other instruments resulted in such works as the *Sonata a quattro* for two horns and two bassoons by Johann Wilhelm Hertel (1727–89). A new development was the appearance of sonatas for piano with easy accompaniment for the violin, as composed by Johann Christian Bach and published in London in 1773. It was for Mozart to place the two instruments on a more equal footing, where they have remained ever since, the piano being joined by other instrumental partners as specified by the composer.

While more and more music was being written for wind instruments, it depended to a great extent on the resources available. Gluck's original version of *Orfeo*, produced in Vienna in 1762, included the old chalumeaux, but in the Paris version of 1774 they were replaced by clarinets, which had been established in the French capital for at least 25 years. When Haydn entered the service of Prince Paul Anton Esterhazy in 1759, the orchestra consisted of 2 flutes, 2 oboes, 1 bassoon, 2 horns and strings, while another bassoon, besides trumpets and timpani, could be co-opted. Hence most of his early symphonies used these instruments, and it was only after the court's acquisition of two more horn players in 1763 that he was sometimes able to incorporate four horns into his works, the first time being in the *Symphony No. 13* of that year. (Some of the woodwind players could play more than one instrument, as they do today, so the two cor anglais required in *No 22 'The Philosopher'* (1764) would have been played by the oboists.) Mozart was also restricted during his early years in Salzburg, and it was after his visits to Mannheim and Paris in 1777–8 that he incorporated clarinets into his symphonies, the first one being *No 31, 'The Paris' Symphony*, written for a *concert spirituel* in 1778. Haydn, although using them in other works, did not write for clarinets in a symphony until his 99th, dating from his visit to London in 1794–5. His *Nelson*

Mass provides an example of orchestration restricted by sheer economic considerations in a time of crisis. Written during wartime in 1798 (and later performed on the occasion of a visit by Lord Nelson to Eisenstadt in 1800), it was originally scored only for strings, three trumpets, timpani and organ. The organ played partly as a continuo instrument and partly as a complete substitute for the woodwind and horns which would otherwise have been included.

The average orchestra around 1800 comprised first and second violins, violas, cellos, double basses, 2 flutes, 2 oboes, 2 clarinets, 2 bassoons, 2 horns, 2 trumpets and 2 timpani. It was generally 'conducted' by the leading violinist with his bow, or, if there was one, sometimes by the keyboard player. (Although the piano was fading out in its orchestral capacity as successor to the harpsichord continuo, it was rapidly gaining ground as a concerto soloist.) Up to this time, the trombone, piccolo and contrabassoon had been called for through the dramatic needs of opera and oratorio, but it was only from the time of Beethoven's *Fifth Symphony* (1805–07) that they became more frequent members of the concert orchestra, being joined in the *Ninth Symphony* (1824) by the triangle, cymbals and bass drum of the 'Turkish' music. Beethoven's achievement was not to introduce new instruments, but to explore to the full the known qualities of those that were

198. A theatre band, directed by its violinist. Behind him are played a serpent, ophicleide, trombone with dragon's head and drum. From 'La Parodie de la Vestale', *Chants et Chansons Populaires de la France*, *II, 1843. London, British Library, Hirsch M.108.*

already there. For instance the double basses, which hitherto had been used mainly to double the cellos in the easier music, were now given some very difficult sections, due to Beethoven's belief that what could be done by Dragonetti might also be done by others. The cellos and violas had more melodic parts than before, and all the bowed strings were made to play in higher positions, not only by Beethoven but also by such contemporaries as Schubert and Weber, whose opera *Der Freischütz* inspired orchestrators for many years to come. Weber was also responsible for the introduction of the third kettledrum, although it was not immediately adopted elsewhere. Four horns became normal, and further use was made of handstopping. It is not certain, however, whether the elaborate solo for fourth horn in the slow movement of Beethoven's *Ninth Symphony* used this technique, or whether it involved an early use of the valved instrument.

In contrast to this there should be mentioned the exploitation of hunting horns in bands, which had already been popular for nearly 50 years before Spohr heard one at St Petersburg in 1803. Describing their context in his autobiography, he wrote:

During Lent, when no public performances are allowed, the Court Theatre gave two big concerts a week in the Steiner Theatre, at which all the virtuosos of the Court Orchestra . . . appeared. The orchestra, at the first concert, consisted of thirty-six violins and twenty basses and doubled winds. In addition to this, and as reinforcement for the chorus, were forty hornists of the Imperial Band, of whom each individual had to play only one tone. They served as an organ, and gave strength and security to the singing of the chorus, whose parts they doubled. In certain small solo passages the effect was overwhelming. Between the first and second parts of the second concerto, these same hornists played an overture of Gluck, with a speed and exactitude that would have been difficult enough for string players and seemed sheerly miraculous as done by hornists, each of them playing only a single tone. It is hardly credible that they could accomplish the most rapid passages with the utmost clarity, and I, for one, would not believe it possible had I not heard it with my own ears. And yet, understandably enough, the adagio of the overture made a greater effect than the allegro for it remains a kind of monstrosity to drill fast passages into these living organ pipes, and one cannot help thinking of the disciplinary methods by which it must have been achieved.

It is to a great extent with wind instruments that the subsequent development of instrumentation is involved. In the early years of the century, orchestras and bands were often reinforced by a serpent, Russian bassoon or bass horn in the lower parts. Of uncertain intonation, they were joined or superseded by the ophicleide after this large form of keyed bugle was patented in 1821. Horns, trumpets and cornets were revolutionized after the invention of valves in Berlin (see page 147), and after Spontini sent some valved instruments to Paris in 1826 they were gradually included in the scores of French composers, one of the earliest instances being a valved trumpet in Berlioz' opera *Les Francs Juges* of 1827.

199. Louis Antoine Jullien conducting his concert orchestra and four military bands at Covent Garden in 1846. *The Illustrated London News,* *7 November 1846.*

Nevertheless it was a long time before they were widely adopted, most players preferring the valveless instruments to which they were accustomed. The invention of the orchestral tuba (complete with valves) around 1835 gave the strongest bass yet to the other brass families, and it was quickly adopted in Germany, taking longer to become established in England and France, where the ophicleide persisted until the 1860s and even then was preserved for a time in outdoor bands (see page 148). In military music new sounds came on the scene with tenor and alto horns, saxhorns and helicons, and a prominent part was given to the cornopean or cornet-à-pistons. Meanwhile the cor anglais, which had previously been used only on rare occasions in the orchestra, now took a more permanent place, a striking acknowledgment being its long solo in the *Roman Carnival* overture by Berlioz. The basset horn, which likewise dated back to the eighteenth century, having often been used by Mozart, was called for by Mendelssohn and a few other composers, but did not become a regular member of the orchestra due to the appearance of the bass clarinet. The saxophone, dating from 1840 and used in certain orchestra works, has been restricted mainly to bands and light music, as has the somewhat later sarrusophone.

200. *A Village Choir* by Thomas Webster (1800–86). The singers are joined by clarinet, bassoon and cello. *London, Victoria and Albert Museum.*

Berlioz was very much concerned with the balance of instrumental forces, realizing that, while the number of strings was fairly static, their relative strength was being reduced due to the increasing number of wind instruments. In his *Treatise on Instrumentation* (1844) he listed the requirements for 'the finest orchestra' as being

21 first violins
20 second violins
18 violas
 8 first violoncellos
 7 second violoncellos
10 double basses
 4 harps
 2 small flutes
 2 large flutes
 2 oboes
 1 English horn
 2 clarinets
 1 basset-horn or 1 bass clarinet
 4 bassoons
 4 valve horns
 2 valve trumpets
 2 cornets with pistons (or cylinders)
 3 trombones (1 alto / 2 tenor) or 3 tenor trombones
 1 bass trombone
 1 ophicleide in B flat (or 1 bass tuba)
 2 pairs of kettledrums with 4 drummers
 1 bass drum
 1 pair of cymbals

Not quite content, he also devised a plan for an orchestra of 465 instrumentalists which would include 30 harps and 30 pianos. Among the different sound effects it might produce, he described

> combining the low tones of the ophicleides, bass tubas and French horns into a small band, joined with the pedal tones of the tenor trombones, the lowest of the bass trombones and the 16' stop of the organ – profoundly grave, religious and calm expression in *piano*

and

> combining the 30 harps with the entire mass of stringed instruments playing pizzicato into a large orchestra, thus forming a new gigantic harp with 934 strings – graceful, brilliant and voluptuous expression in all shadings

besides

> combining the 30 pianofortes with the 6 sets of small bells, the 12 pairs of ancient cymbals, the 6 triangles (which might be tuned in different keys like cymbals) and the 4 crescents into a metallic percussion orchestra – gay and brilliant expression in *mezzoforte*

and

> combining the French horns, trumpets, cornets, trombones and ophicleides into a small band – pompous and brilliant expression in *forte*.

(For this 'small band' there were 16 French horns of which 6 were to have valves, 8 trumpets, 6 cornets, 4 alto trombones, 6 tenor trombones, 2 bass trombones and 3 ophicleides.) This orchestra never came into existence, as it was only intended to be tried out for one performance, and, as Berlioz said, it would have needed a specially designed hall built for the occasion. On seeing the care taken over his treatise, one can imagine his frustrations when, at a party in Vienna, he heard his *Roman Carnival* overture

> arranged for two pianos (eight hands) and physharmonica. When its turn came, I was near the door which opened onto the room where the five performers were seated. They began the first allegro much too slowly. The andante was passable; but the moment the allegro was resumed, at an even more dragging pace than before, I turned scarlet, the blood rushed to my head and, unable to contain my impatience, I shouted out: 'This is the carnival, not Lent. You make it sound like Good Friday in Rome'. The hilarity of the audience at this outburst may be imagined. It was impossible to restore silence, and the rest of the overture was performed in a buzz of laughter and conversation, amid which my five interpreters pursued their placid course imperturbably to the end.

(Berlioz, *Memoirs*)

Berlioz was unique in his use of instruments and his theories as to what could be done with them. Other composers of his time were not so *avant-garde* in this respect, and advanced at a steadier pace. Wagner, for instance, called not so much for a wide variety of instruments as for larger numbers of each than were customary, with great emphasis on the brass. (In his early works he wrote for natural

201. The Crediton Town Band in 1862, photographed by William Hector (1810–82). *Collection of Gordon Hector, Esq., Weymouth.*

and valved horns together, but he later discarded the valveless type.) In *Die Walküre* (composed in 1854–6), to take one example, he specified, apart from a large number of strings and woodwind, 8 horns, 4 trumpets, 6 trombones and 5 tubas, besides 6 harps. In contrast to this, Brahms and Dvořák used orchestras little larger than that of Beethoven (the chief addition being that of the tuba), although by writing at a later date they were able to profit by a greater use of valved instruments in general, and by the more highly developed woodwind.

The latter part of the nineteenth century saw an increase in the use of percussion instruments, represented chiefly by castanets in Spanish-type pieces, by gongs, and by the tuned percussion. Descriptive music of the Romantic age often required the use of bells, a striking example being Rimsky-Korsakov's *Russian Easter Overture* (1888), where *campanelli* are specified. In his *Principles of Orchestration* (on which he was working at the time of his death in 1908) the composer suggests that this effect is best obtained by the glockenspiel of steel bars; for deeper-sounding bells, as also required in the overture, a tamtam is used. In the treatise Rimsky-Korsakov wrote that 'real church bells of moderate size may be considered more as theatrical properties than orchestral instruments'. From this period, too, there can be seen greater use of the xylophone and celesta, and the appearance of tubular bells.

Twentieth-century instrumentation reflects the developments described in chapter X. At the turn of the century there were vast Teutonic orchestras which reached a peak in Mahler's *Eighth Symphony* (1907), scored for voices, strings and

4 flutes	1 bass drum
2 piccolos	cymbals
4 oboes	1 gong
1 English horn	1 triangle
3 clarinets	deep bells
2 E flat clarinets	1 glockenspiel
1 bass clarinet	1 celesta
4 bassoons	1 piano
1 contra-bassoon	1 harmonium
8 horns	1 organ
8 trumpets (4 offstage)	2 harps
7 trombones (3 offstage)	1 mandoline
1 bass tuba	
timpani	

This was exceptional, but large scoring for traditional instruments has continued to this day in the works of such composers as Stravinsky, Shostakovitch and Messiaen. In complete contrast are such pieces for small orchestra as Stravinsky's *Histoire du Soldat* (1918), which uses only one violin, double bass, clarinet, bassoon, cornet, trombone, and eight percussion instruments played by one person. The quest for new sounds led him to plan music for *Les Noces* for 'a mechanical piano, an electrically-driven harmonium, an ensemble of percussion instruments and two Hungarian cymbaloms', according to his *Chronicle of My Life*. Only after writing a good deal of the music did he realize that there would be difficulties in synchronizing mechanical instruments with live performers, and the idea was abandoned. The general increase of percussion instruments, largely due to importations from Africa and the East, and to the ingenuity of such masters as James Blades, has greatly augmented the sound repertoire. A *gamelan* of percussion instruments appears in Messiaen's *Turangalila Symphony* (1948), together with a large traditional orchestra joined by a solo piano, a vibraphone and ondes Martenot. A comparatively recent scoring for small orchestra is the *Eclat* by Boulez (1965), for

Piano	Mandoline	Cor anglais
Celesta	Guitar	Trumpet
Harp	Cymbalum	Trombone
Glockenspiel	Tubular bells	Viola
Vibraphone	Flute	Violoncello

202. A Duo-Art Pianola piano playing with the Queen's Hall Orchestra under Sir Henry Wood in 1922 (in spite of the qualms of Stravinsky, noted above. *The Illustrated London News, 11 November 1922.*

203.   The B.B.C. Symphony Orchestra, conducted by Pierre Boulez in the
Royal Festival Hall, London, on 8 November 1972.

This scoring seems to be relatively traditional when compared to Stockhausen's
Ylem, where conventional instruments are joined by an electronic organ, electric
cello, electronium, synthesizer and electric-Sax-synthesizer. Both orchestral and
chamber works use the new methods of playing traditional instruments as
described on page 187, indicated by signs which are frequently more reminiscent
of the Highway Code than of music. It is small wonder that, at a London rehearsal
of a very *avant-garde* orchestral piece in 1968, a well-known double-bass player
made the occasion memorable by calling out to the conductor 'Am I supposed to
be playing the same thing as my neighbour?'. He was not.

It is fitting to end with a subject which gives pure fun to musicians and audiences

204. The Band of the Royal Regiment of Artillery at the Royal Artillery Barracks, Woolwich, in July 1970.

alike. Musical jokes have been played for centuries, often using unusual instruments such as the **nightingale, cuckoo, quail** and **rattle** which appear among the soloists in the *Toy Symphony* formerly attributed to Joseph Haydn, but now thought to be the combined work of Leopold Mozart and Michael Haydn. When, therefore, Antony Hopkins wrote his *Concerto for Two Tuning Forks in the C & A Modes* for the annual 'At Home' of the Royal College of Music on 15 June 1956, he was doing so in a very worthy tradition. Meanwhile, Gerard Hoffnung, the artist and tuba-player, was entertaining thousands of people with his cartoons of musicians and their instruments, and, also in 1956, their spirit came to life around the originator in the first of several Hoffnung Concerts, held on 13

205. Three vacuum cleaners and a floor polisher, played by the Amadeus Quartet (Norbert Brainin, Sigmund Nissel, Peter Schidloff and Martin Lovett) in Malcolm Arnold's *Grand Grand Overture*, a work written for the Hoffnung Music Festival in 1956. This picture was taken during the performance on 14 December 1976, in the Royal Albert Hall, London.

November in the Royal Festival Hall, London. Denis Brain played on a hosepipe the solo part in Leopold Mozart's *Concerto for Alphorn and Strings*, Malcolm Arnold's *Grand Grand Overture* included prominent parts for Hoover **vacuum cleaners** and a **floor polisher**, and the distinguished actress Yvonne Arnaud was the soloist in Franz Reizenstein's *Concerto Popolare* (a brilliant combination of material from some of the best-known piano concertos), finally throwing her knitting at Norman Del Mar, the conductor, and receiving after it all a bouquet of cauliflowers. Hoffnung himself displayed his genius with his 'Stradivarius tuba. . . . by Boosey and Hawkes'. His untimely death at the age of 34 caused these concerts gradually to diminish in number, but they have been recorded, and together with his books of cartoons give pleasure to musicians and music-lovers across the globe. They, and the work of other inspired musical humorists, give tonic to a world which needs to be revived.

Glossary

The words given here are those which are not described in the text, or else occur several times with the description only once.

ACTION   In keyboard instruments, the mechanism linking a key with its string(s) or pipe(s).

BARRING   Strips of wood supporting a soundboard from below, and helping to transmit vibrations received from the strings.

BELL   The expanding end of certain wind instruments.

BOUTS   In the viol, violin and guitar families, the sections caused by the curving of the sides, i.e. upper, middle and lower bouts.

CHANTER   The part of a bagpipe upon which the melody is played.

CHROMATIC   Notes foreign to a given major or minor scale.

CONTINUO (BASSO CONTINUO)   The bass line of many Baroque compositions, generally figured to indicate the harmonies above. (See FIGURED BASS)

COURSE   A string, or strings tuned at the unison or octave, as set in the lute, dulcimer, harpsichord, etc.

CROOK   An extra length of tubing which a) lowers the basic note of wind instruments, or b) holds the double reed of the bassoon, rackett, etc.

DIAPASON PIPES   Flue pipes, open or stopped, which give the characteristic tone of an organ.

DIATONIC   The notes of a given major or minor scale.

DOMINANT   The fifth note of a scale.

DOUBLE STOPPING   The simultaneous performance of two or more notes on a stringed instrument.

DRONE   A long sustained note held against one or more faster moving parts, as on the bagpipe.

EMBOUCHURE   The position of a player's mouth in playing a wind instrument.

ESCAPEMENT   A device in the piano which enables the hammer to fall back from the string while the key is still depressed.

FONTANELLE   A perforated barrel used to cover part of a key in large woodwind instruments from the late mediaeval to early Baroque periods.

FIGURED BASS   A bass line under which figures indicate the chords to be played above.

FLUE PIPE   A pipe with a narrow duct or windway.

FRET   A line of gut, wood or metal, indicating where notes can be obtained on certain stringed instruments.

GLISSANDO   The rapid ascent or descent of a given interval, sounding as a fast scale on instruments of prepared pitch, e.g. harp or piano, and as a slide on others, e.g. violin or trombone.

HETEROPHONY   A melody performed slightly differently by two or more people at once.

MANUAL   A keyboard.

MEAN, MEANE
a) a viol playing a middle part;
b) one of the viol's middle strings.

MIXTURE STOP   A composite organ stop comprising two or more ranks, some of which are overtones.

MUTATION STOP   An organ stop which gives an overtone without its fundamental.

ORGANUM (PARALLEL)   A mediaeval technique of composition in which two or more parts proceed in parallel motion, normally at the fourth, fifth or octave above a plainsong melody.

PALLET   A device which when at rest prevents air from entering an organ pipe, and when pulled down, as the result of a key being depressed, lets it through.

POLYPHONY   Music consisting of two or more independent parts performed together.

RANK   A set of organ pipes of the same tonal quality.

REGISTER
a) The upper, middle or lower range of a voice or instrument.
b) See RANK.

REGISTRATION   The selection of ranks or registers.

ROLLER   A rolling device in the organ mechanism, by which contact is made between the key and the pallet.

SCORDATURA   The irregular tuning of a bowed instrument to facilitate double stopping.

STOP (noun)
a) An organ or harpsichord rank or register.
b) The handle which when pulled makes the rank playable.

STOP (verb)   To determine the pitch by
a) pressing the fingers onto a string;
b) blocking the end of a pipe.

SWELL   a) A device for causing *crescendo* and *diminuendo* on the organ and late harpsichord. b) The organ department and manual from which these effects can be obtained.

SYMPATHETIC STRINGS   Metal strings which are unstopped by the fingers and vibrate in sympathy with those which are bowed.

TAILPIECE   A piece of wood or ebony to which the strings are attached at the lower end of the viol and violin families, and also in certain earlier instruments, whether plucked or bowed.

TONIC   The keynote of a scale.

TRANSPOSING INSTRUMENTS   Those which have music written at one pitch but sound at another.

VALVE (on brass instruments)   A built-in device which when pressed changes the available length of tubing.

WRESTPLANK   In keyboard instruments, the plank in which tuning pins are set.

Bibliography

CHAPTERS I AND II. *Stringed Instruments, Plucked and Bowed*

Andersson, Otto: *The Bowed Harp*, London, 1930.

Bachmann, Werner: *The Origins of Bowing*, transl. Norma Deane, London, 1969.

Bellow, Alexander: *The Illustrated History of the Guitar*, New York, 1970.

Boyden, David D.: *The History of Violin Playing from its Origins to 1761*, London, 1965.

Boyden, David D.: *The Hill Collection*, London, New York, Toronto, 1969.

Cowling, Elizabeth: *The Cello*, London, Sydney, 1975.

Danks, Harry: *The Viola d'amore*, Bois de Boulogne, 1976.

Dolmetsch, Nathalie: *The Viola da Gamba*, London, New York, Frankfurt, 3rd edn., 1975.

Gill, Donald: *Gut-strung Plucked Instruments contemporary with the Lute*, Lute Society, 1976.

Grunfeld, Frederic V.: *The Art and Times of the Guitar*, New York, London, 1969.

Harwood, Ian: *A Brief History of the Lute*, Lute Society, 1975.

Hayes, Gerald R.: *The Viols and Other Bowed Instruments*, London, 1930, reprint New York, 1969.

Heron-Allen, Edward: *Violin-Making as it was and is*, 2nd edn., London, Melbourne, Cape Town, 1885/6.

The Lute Society Journal, London, 1959–.

Mace, Thomas: *Musick's Monument*, London, 1676. Reprint, Paris, 1958.

Mozart, Leopold: *A Treatise on the Fundamental Principles of Violin Playing* (*Versuch einer gründlichen Violinschule*, Augsburg, 1756), transl. Editha Knocker, London, New York, Toronto, 1951.

Nelson, Sheila M.: *The Violin Family*, London, 1964.

Nelson, Sheila M.: *The Violin and Viola*, London, New York, 1972.

Panum, Hortense: *Stringed Instruments of the Middle Ages*, transl. Jeffrey Pulver, London, 1941.

Remnant, Mary: *Bowed Instruments in England up to the Reformation*, unpublished D.Phil. thesis, University of Oxford, 1972.

Rensch, Roslyn: *The Harp*, London, 1969.

Retford, William C.: *Bows and Bow Makers*, London, 1964.

Rimmer, Joan: *The Irish Harp*, Dublin, 1969.

Roberts, Ronald: *Making a simple Violin and Viola*, Newton Abbot, London, North Pomfret (Vt), Vancouver, 1975.

Turnbull, Harvey: *The Guitar from the Renaissance to the Present Day*, London, 1974.

Winternitz, Emanuel: 'The Survival of the Kithara and the Evolution of the English Cittern: A Study in Morphology', *Musical Instruments and their Symbolism in Western Art*, London, 1967, 57–65.

Winternitz, Emanuel: *Gaudenzio Ferrari, His School, and the Early History of the Violin*, Varallo Sesia, 1967.

Woodfield, Ian: *The Origins of the Viol*, unpublished Ph.D. thesis, University of London, 1977.

CHAPTERS III AND IV. *String Keyboard Instruments and Organs*

Andersen, Poul-Gerhard: *Organ Building and Design*, transl. Joanne Curnutt, London, 1969.

Blanchard, Homer H.: *Organs of our Time*, Delaware, Ohio, 1975.

Boalch, Donald H.: *Makers of the Harpsichord and Clavichord 1440–1840*, rev. edn., Oxford, 1974.

Closson, Ernest: *History of the Piano*, transl. Delano Ames, rev. by Robin Golding, London, 1974.

Clutton, Cecil, and Niland, Austin: *The British Organ*, London, 1963.

Erlich, Cyril: *The Piano*, London, 1976.

Haacke, Walter: *Organs of the World*, London, 1966.

Harding, Rosamond: *The Piano-Forte, its History traced to the Great Exhibition of 1851*, Cambridge, 1933.

Hirt, Franz Josef: *Stringed Keyboard Instruments 1440–1880*, Boston, Mass., 1968.

Hollis, Helen Rice: *The Piano*, Newton Abbot, London, Vancouver, 1975.

Hubbard, Frank: *Three Centuries of Harpsichord Making*, Harvard, 1965.

James, Philip: *Early Keyboard Instruments*, London, 1930.

Klotz, Hans: *The Organ Handbook*, transl. Gerhard Krapf, Saint Louis, London, 1969.

Michel, N.E.: *Historical Pianos, Clavichords and Harpsichords*, Poco Rivera, Calif., [1963].

Niland, Austin: *Introduction to the Organ*, London, 1968.

The Organ Yearbook, Buren (Gld.), 1970–.

Perrot, Jean: *The Organ from its Invention in the Hellenistic Period to the end of the Thirteenth Century*, transl. Norma Deane, London, New York, Toronto, 1971.

Ripin, Edwin, ed.: *Keyboard Instruments*, Edinburgh, Chicago, 1971.

Russell, Raymond: *The Harpsichord and Clavichord*, 2nd edn., rev. by Howard Schott, London, 1973.

Russell, Raymond: *Victoria and Albert Museum: Catalogue of Musical Instruments, Vol. 1, Keyboard Instruments*, London, 1968.

Sumner, William Leslie: *The Organ*, 3rd edn., rev., London, 1962.

Sumner, William Leslie: *The Pianoforte*, London, 1966.

Van Barthold, Kenneth, and Buckton, David: *The Story of the Piano*, London, 1975.

Wainwright, David: *The Piano Makers*, London, 1975.

Walcker-Mayer, Werner: *The Roman Organ of Aquincum*, Ludwigsburg, 1972.

Wilson, Michael: *The English Chamber Organ*, Oxford, 1968.

Williams, Peter: *The European Organ 1450–1850*, London, 1966.

Zuckermann, Wolfgang: *The Modern Harpsichord*, New York, 1969.

CHAPTERS V, VI AND VII. *Woodwind, Brass and Free Reed Instruments*

Altenburg, Johann Ernst: *The Trumpeters' and Kettledrummers' Art (Trompeter und Pauker-Kunst*, Halle, 1795), transl. Edward H. Tarr, Nashville, 1974.

Baines, Anthony: *Brass Instruments: Their History and Development*, London, 1976.

Baines, Anthony: *Woodwind Instruments and their History*, 2nd edn., London, 1962.

Baines, Anthony: *Bagpipes*, Oxford, 1960.

Bate, Philip: *The Flute*, London, New York, 1969.

Bate, Philip: *The Oboe*, 3rd edn., London, 1975.

Bate, Philip: *The Trumpet and Trombone*, London, New York, 1966.

The Brass Quarterly and *The Brass and Woodwind Quarterly*, 1957–.

Brüchle, Bernhard, and Janetsky, Kurt: *A Pictorial History of the Horn*, Tutzing, 1976.

Collinson, Francis: *The Bagpipe*, London and Boston, 1975.

Fitzpatrick, Horace: *The Horn and Horn-Playing . . . from 1680 to 1830*, London, New York, Toronto, 1970.

Gregory, Robin: *The Horn*, 2nd edn., London, 1969.

Gregory, Robin: *The Trombone*, London, 1973.

Hohner, M., Ltd.: *The Happy Harmonica*, New York.

Hunt, Edgar: *The Recorder and its Music*, London, 1962.

Langwill, Lyndesay G.: *An Index of Musical Wind-Instrument Makers*, 4th edn., Edinburgh, 1974.

Langwill, Lyndesay G.: *The Bassoon and Contra-Bassoon*, London, New York, 1965.

Menke, Werner: *History of the Trumpet of Bach and Handel*, trans. Gerald Abraham, Nashville, 1972.

Morley-Pegge, R.: *The French Horn*, 2nd edn., London, New York, 1973.

Quantz, Johann Joachim: *On Playing the Flute (Versuch einer Anweisung die Flöte traversière zu spielen*, Berlin, 1752), transl. and introd. by Edward R. Reilly, London, 1966.

Rendall, F. Geoffrey: *The Clarinet*, 3rd edn., rev. by Philip Bate, London, New York, 1971.

Ridley, E. A. K.: *Wind Instruments of European Art Music*, London (Horniman Museum), 1974.

Rockstro, R. S.: *A Treatise on the Construction, History and Practice of the Flute*, transl. G. M. Rockstro, London, 1890, 1928.

Smithers, Don: *The Music and History of the Baroque Trumpet before 1721*, London, 1973.

Welch, Christopher: *Lectures on the Recorder*, introd. by Edgar Hunt, London, New York, Toronto, 1961.

Welch, Christopher: *The History of the Boehm Flute*, 3rd edn, London, New York, 1896.

CHAPTERS VIII, IX AND X. *Percussion, Mechanical and Twentieth century Instruments*

Blades, James: *Percussion Instruments and their History*, 2nd edn, London, 1975.

Blades, James, and Montagu, Jeremy: *Early Percussion Instruments*, London, 1976.

Boston, Canon Noel, and Langwill, Lyndesay, G.: *Church and Chamber Barrel Organs*, Edinburgh, 1967.

Buchner, Alexander: *Mechanical Musical Instruments*, transl. Iris Urwin, London, 1959.

Clark, John E.T., *Musical Boxes*, 2nd edn, London, 1952.

Dorf, Richard H.: *Electronic Musical Instruments*, 3rd edn., New York, 1968.

Douglas, Alan: *Electronic Music Production*, Bath, 1973.

Hoover, Cynthia A.: *Music Machines – American Style*, Washington D.C., 1971.

Kettlewell, David: *The Dulcimer*, unpublished Ph.D. thesis, University of Technology, Loughborough, 1977.

Ord-Hume, Arthur: *Player Piano*, London, 1970.

Ord-Hume, Arthur: *Clockwork Music*, London, 1973.

Peinkofer, Karl, and Tannigel, Fritz: *Handbook of Percussion Instruments*, transl. by Kurt and Else Stone, London, New York, Mainz, 1976.

Risatti, Howard: *New Music Vocabulary*, Urbana, Chicago, London, 1975.

Sear, Walter: *The New World of Electronic Music*, New York, 1972.

Smith Brindle, Reginald: *Contemporary Percussion*, London, New York, Toronto, 1970.

Tallis, David: *Musical Boxes*, London, 1971.

Webb, Graham: *The Disc Musical Box Handbook*, London, 1971.

CHAPTER XI. *The Development of Instrumentation*

Adkins, H.E.: *Treatise on the Military Band*, 2nd rev. edn, London, 1958.

Berlioz, Hector: *Treatise on Instrumentation* (*Traité de l'Instrumentation*, Paris, 1844), rev. by Richard Strauss, transl. Theodore Front, New York, 1948.

Carse, Adam: *The History of Orchestration*, London, 1925, New York, 1964.

Carse, Adam: *The Orchestra in the XVIIIth Century*, Cambridge, 1940.

Carse, Adam: *The Orchestra from Beethoven to Berlioz*, London, 1948.

Dart, Thurston: *The Interpretation of Music*, London, 1954.

Landon, H.C. Robbins: *Haydn Symphonies*, London, 1966.

Landon, H.C. Robbins: *The Symphonies of Joseph Haydn*, London, 1955.

Forsyth, Cecil: *Orchestration*, 2nd edn., London, 1935.

Nettel, Reginald: *The Orchestra in England*, 2nd edn, London, 1956.

Minor, Andrew C., and Mitchell, Bonner: *A Renaissance Entertainment*, Columbia, Missouri, 1968.

Piston, Walter: *Orchestration*, London, 1971.

Rimsky-Korsakov, Nikolay: *Principles of Orchestration*, ed. Maximilian Steinberg, transl. Edward Agate, 1922, reprint New York, 1964.

Selfridge-Field, Eleanor: *Venetian Instrumental Music from Gabrieli to Vivaldi*, Oxford, 1975.

Terry, Charles Sanford: *Bach's Orchestra*, London, 1932.

GENERAL

Baines, Anthony: *European and American Musical Instruments*, London, 1966.

Baines, Anthony: *Musical Instruments through the Ages*, Harmondsworth, 3rd edn, 1969.

Baines, Anthony: *Victoria and Albert Museum, Catalogue of Musical Instruments. Vol. II. Non-Keyboard Instruments*, London, 1968.

Berlioz *The Memoirs of Hector Berlioz,* trans. & ed. David Cairns, London, 1969.

Berner, A., van der Meer, J.H. and Thibault, G.: *Preservation and Restoration of Musical Instruments*, London, 1967.

Bessaraboff, Nicholas: *Ancient European Musical Instruments*, New York, 1941.

Bonanni, Filippo: *The Showcase of Musical Instruments* (*Gabinetto Armonico*, Rome, 1723), ed. Frank Ll. Harrison and Joan Rimmer, New York, 1964.

Bragard, Roger, and de Hen, Ferdinand: *Musical Instruments in Art and History*, transl. Bill Hopkins, London, 1968.

Buchner, Alexander: *Musical Instruments through the Ages*, transl. Iris Urwin, London, 1955.

Burney: *Dr. Burney's Musical Tours in Europe*, ed. Percy A. Scholes, 2 vols., London, 1959.

Carter, Henry Holland: *A Dictionary of Middle English Musical Terms*, Indiana, 1961.

Clemencic, René: *Old Musical Instruments*, trans. David Hermges, London, 1968.

Crane, Frederick: *Extant Medieval Musical Instruments*, Iowa, 1972.

Donington, Robert: *The Instruments of Music*, 3rd edn, London, 1970.

Early Music, London, 1973–.

Fellowship of Makers and Restorers of Historical Instruments: Bulletin and Communications, London.

Fox, Lilla M.: *Instruments of the Orchestra*, London, 1971.

Galpin, Canon Francis W.: *Old English Instruments of Music*, 4th edn, rev. Thurston Dart, London, 1965.

Galpin Society Journal, The, London.

Geiringer, Karl: *Musical Instruments*, 2nd edn, London, 1945.

Grove's Dictionary of Music and Musicians, 5th edn, ed. Eric Blom, London, 1954.

Harrison, Frank, and Rimmer, Joan: *European Musical Instruments*, Lon., 1964.

Marcuse, Sibyl: *Musical Instruments: a Comprehensive Dictionary*, N. York, 1964.

Marcuse, Sibyl: *A Survey of Musical Instruments*, Newton Abbot, London, 1975.

Mersenne, Marin: *Harmonie Universelle*, Paris, 1636. Latin edn (*Harmonicorum libri*, Paris, 1635), transl. R.E. Chapman, The Hague, 1957.

Montagu, Jeremy: *The World of Medieval and Renaissance Musical Instruments*, Newton Abbot, London, Vancouver, 1976.

Mozart: *Mozart's Letters*, ed. Eric Blom, London, 1956; selected from *The Letters of Mozart and his Family*, transl. and annotated by Emily Anderson, London, 1938.

Munrow, David: *Instruments of the Middle Ages and Renaissance*, London, 1976.

North: *Roger North on Music*, transcribed and ed. John Wilson, London, 1959.

Pepys: *The Diary of Samuel Pepys*, transcribed and ed. by Robert Latham and William Matthews, London, 1970–.

Praetorius: *The Syntagma Musicum of Michael Praetorius*, transl. Harold Blumenfeld, 1949, 1962. (Selections from 'De Organographia', 1619, and 'Theatrum Instrumentorum', 1620.)

Pulver, Jeffrey: *A Dictionary of Old English Music and Musical Instruments*, London, 1923.

Rimmer, Joan: *Ancient Musical Instruments of Western Asia*, London (British Museum), 1969.

Roberts, Ronald: *Musical Instruments Made to be Played*, 2nd edn, Leicester, 1967.

Royal Musical Association, Proceedings of the, London, 1874–.

Sachs, Curt: *The History of Musical Instruments*, New York, 1940.

Spohr: *The Musical Journeys of Louis Spohr*, transl. and ed. by Henry Pleasants, Oklahoma, 1961.

Tinctoris: Anthony Baines, 'Fifteenth-century Instruments in Tinctoris's *De Inventione et Usu Musicae*', GSJ III (1950), 19–26.

Thibault, G., Jenkins, Jean, Bran-Ricci, Josiane: *Eighteenth Century Musical Instruments: France and Britain*, London (Victoria and Albert Museum), 1973.

The Triumph of Maximilian I, transl. and ed. by Stanley Appelbaum, New York (Dover Publications Inc.), 1964.

Winternitz, Emanuel: *Musical Instruments of the Western World*, London, 1966.

Winternitz, Emanuel: *Musical Instruments and their Symbolism in Western Art*, London, 1967.

Index

Due to the vast scope of this book the Index is necessarily selective, and cannot list all the instruments, makers and writers referred to. Instruments not mentioned specifically may, however, be traced through their generic group.